The Last Christians

The Last Christians

Stories of Persecution, Flight, and Resilience in the Middle East

Andreas Knapp

Translated by Sharon Howe

Plough Publishing House

Published by Plough Publishing House
Walden, New York
Robertsbridge, England
Elsmore, Australia
www.plough.com

Plough produces books, a quarterly magazine, and Plough.com to encourage people and help them put their faith into action. We believe Jesus can transform the world and that his teachings and example apply to all aspects of life. At the same time, we seek common ground with all people regardless of their creed.

Plough is the publishing house of the Bruderhof, an international community of families and singles seeking to follow Jesus together. Members of the Bruderhof are committed to a way of radical discipleship in the spirit of the Sermon on the Mount. Inspired by the first church in Jerusalem (Acts 2 and 4), they renounce private property and share everything in common in a life of nonviolence, justice, and service to neighbors near and far. To learn more about the Bruderhof's faith, history, and daily life, see Bruderhof.com. (Views expressed by Plough authors are their own and do not necessarily reflect the position of the Bruderhof.)

ISBN: 978-0-87486-062-7
22 21 20 19 18 17   1 2 3 4 5 6 7 8

Originally published in German as *Die letzten Christen: Flucht und Vertreibung aus dem Nahen Osten* by Andreas Knapp, Copyright © 2016 by adeo Verlag, Gerth Medien GmbH, Asslar, Germany. All dialogues and stories are authentic, but some names, locations, and circumstances have been changed to protect the individuals concerned.

Cover photograph: Louai Beshara/AFP/Getty Images

A catalog record for this book is available from the British Library.
Library of Congress Cataloging-in-Publication Data

Names: Knapp, Andreas, (Catholic priest), author. | Howe, Sharon, translator.
Title: The last Christians : stories of persecution, flight, and resilience
  in the Middle East / Andreas Knapp ; translated by Sharon Howe.
Other titles: Letzten Christen. English
Description: Walden : Plough Publishing House, 2017. | Includes
  bibliographical references.
Identifiers: LCCN 2017024389 (print) | LCCN 2017029570 (ebook) | ISBN
  9780874860702 (epub) | ISBN 9780874860719 (mobi) | ISBN 9780874860733 (
  pdf) | ISBN 9780874860627 (hardcover)
Subjects: LCSH: Persecution--Middle East--History--21st century. |
  Christians--Middle East--History--21st century. | IS (Organization)
Classification: LCC BR1608.M628 (ebook) | LCC BR1608.M628 K5313 2017 (print)
  | DDC 272.0956--dc23
LC record available at https://lccn.loc.gov/2017024389

Printed in the United States of America

Contents

Preface

Giving a Voice to the Voiceless

For a long time Christians in the Middle East have been condemned to silence. For centuries they have been discriminated against by a predominantly Muslim society and, as a minority, they have been forced to quietly accept injustice and lead an inconspicuous life in the shadows. Even I, a priest and theologian, was for a long time unaware of the moving story of Christians in Syria and Iraq.

Those who are now coming to the West as refugees find themselves voiceless once again, having not yet learned our language. And sometimes Christians in refugee camps are obliged to deny their identity to avoid being exposed to further attacks by radical Muslims.

Two years ago, I met some Christians from the Middle East who now live in my neighborhood of Grünau in Leipzig, Germany. Having listened to their stories, I was so moved I had to write them down. They may not be entirely politically correct, but they are correct in the sense that they are authentic. Sometimes my closeness to these victims of persecution and displacement causes me to feel a sense of powerlessness, grief, or indignation. At the same time, I know that the experiences of Iraqi and Syrian Christians are only a fragment in the great mosaic of world history. I could have set their view of Islam in the context of many other, widely differing perspectives. But I have chosen to focus on this small fragment precisely because it has so often been suppressed and neglected. Only by embracing the history and stories of Christians from the Middle East can we begin to do justice to an increasingly complex reality. And only by exercising solidarity with victims of all kinds of violence will we come a step closer to a lasting peace.

I would like to thank the staff of Plough and of my German publisher, adeo – especially Stefan Wiesner, Dorothea Bühler, and Gudrun Webel – for their cooperation and support. Special thanks are due to Melanie Wolfers and Michael Lück for their critical eye and many helpful tips. And I remain hugely indebted to the Syrian and Iraqi Christians who shared their stories with me. To them, and to all Christians in the Middle East who have been persecuted or murdered for their faith, I dedicate this book.

1

Looking Death in the Eye

The high barbed-wire fences glint in the yellowish floodlight.
The security measures at the Erbil airport set my nerves
on edge, reminding me how explosive the situation is here.
Fortunately, things are currently calm in the Kurdish autonomous region, but it could be the calm before the storm.

I check my phone: it's three in the morning on Saturday,
November 7, 2015. After numerous security gates, I have
finally emerged from the airport building. I rub my eyes,
not just because I've been up all night, but because I never
would have dreamed three days ago that I'd be traveling to
northern Iraq. And yet here I am, looking out into a dark
landscape punctuated with barbed wire and rows of lights.
What in heaven's name made me come here?

Lightning flashes in the distance. The low rumble of
thunder sounds like gunfire. The front between the autonomous region of Iraqi Kurdistan and the Islamic State (IS)
fighters isn't far from here. Since the fall, the Kurdish peshmerga have been advancing in order to seize back the city
of Sinjar from the IS militia. Peshmerga means "those who
look death in the eye."

That's not quite what I have in mind, even if I am here to
attend a funeral. Beside me is my friend Yousif, whose father
died three days ago. Yousif runs his right hand through his
close-cropped black hair and I hear it crackle.

"Where the hell has my brother got to? Those damn checkpoints," he mutters impatiently, while I shift from one foot to the other. It's not cold, but I'm feeling pretty nervous. There's a strange cawing sound overhead. I look up but can't make out anything in the milky blend of night sky and artificial lighting. Yousif follows my gaze. "Birds," he explains. What kind of birds fly here at night? And what made *me* fly here, for that matter – to a country that carries a State Department travel warning, and for which you can't get a tourist visa? It all seems so unreal to me at this too-early hour of the morning.

Abu Yousif's funeral is due to take place today. What Yousif would have given to see his father again while he was still alive! Two years ago, Yousif was forced to abandon his seriously ill parent – confined to a wheelchair by bone cancer – in Mosul, in order to bring his own wife and their two children to safety. "I want to see my father one more time before he dies," he kept saying. Once he even asked casually, "Will you come with me to Iraq?" And I replied, equally casually, "Why not? Sure I'll come." But now it's no longer just small talk – it's for real. And it happened so quickly.

Last Monday, Yousif applied to the immigration office in Leipzig for a passport to visit his dying father in Iraq. He had planned to fly out just after New Year's. Then, last Wednesday afternoon, I felt my phone vibrate in my pocket and took it out to read, "My father has just died."

Yousif lives just one block down from us in our prefab housing project on the outskirts of Leipzig. I go to see him right away. His twelve-year-old son Amanuel opens the door. Beside him is his sister Shaba, two years younger.

"I'm so sorry to hear about your granddad dying."

They both look at me aghast.

Yousif appears in the hallway. He has heard my words, and raises his bushy eyebrows.

"I haven't told the kids yet."

"Oh, no!" I exclaim, clapping my hands to my face. "I'm sorry . . ."

"It's OK," Yousif continues, putting his arms around both children and reiterating, "Granddad's dead."

At this point Tara, Yousif's stunningly beautiful wife, comes out of the kitchen and everybody cries. My eyes, too, fill with tears, partly out of shame at my own clumsiness.

We sit down in the living room. Yousif starts reproaching himself – "Why didn't I fly out earlier . . ."

I reassure him. "You did everything you could. You only applied for your passport last Monday – no one could have guessed your father would die so soon."

Yousif looks up: "Now my father is in heaven."

Then, pulling himself together, he gets to his feet.

"I'll try and get a flight next Tuesday. I have an important appointment at the job center on Monday, about my first employment contract in Germany."

I make a split-second decision: "OK, Tuesday it is . . . and if it's doable, I'll come with you."

Back home, I sit up late browsing through the website of the Iraqi embassy and consulate. It turns out I can't get a tourist visa, only a business visa, which has to be approved by the Ministry of Interior in Baghdad. I go to bed half disappointed, half relieved. My trip to Iraq is off.

The next morning, I phone the embassy just in case. No chance of a visa. Without getting my hopes up, but just to make sure I've left no stone unturned, I call the consulate in Iraq too. This yields some surprising information: if I only want to travel to the "autonomous region of Kurdistan," there's a special phone number I can try. Game on again!

Yousif answers the phone when I call. Coincidentally, his job appointment has been postponed, and now he wants to move the flight up to Saturday. That way he can attend his father's funeral on Sunday. He has already been to the immigration office and can collect his passport tomorrow. With any luck, it should work out.

On Friday morning, Yousif calls me from the immigration office. He has just been handed his passport.

I have to leave urgently for my regular Friday session at the prison where I do chaplaincy work, but we still need to buy our airline tickets. That would take no time at all online, but neither Yousif nor I have a credit card. I call Stefan Wiesner, the director of a Christian book publisher. We had recently spoken about doing a book on the subject of refugees, and I had mentioned my idea of accompanying Yousif to Iraq next year. "I want to fly to Kurdistan tomorrow," I say. "Can you help me?"

Mr. Wiesner and his assistant take care of everything. It works like a dream.

I spend all day at the prison. In the evening, I attend a discussion group at a local university's Catholic student society. There, I manage to get online and try to print the tickets, but fail. Luckily a student helps me out, and we're back in business.

At nine o'clock I return home. I get on the phone to cancel a couple of appointments. I also have some counseling sessions booked at the prison, but they can wait. I ask my Protestant colleague to notify the prisoners of the new dates. I'm sure it will be fine.

At ten o'clock I pack my small knapsack and slip in a book about Christians in Iraq I've been meaning to read for ages. Then I call Yousif, and we agree to meet tomorrow morning just before six at the train station. As long as the trains aren't on strike, everything should be fine.

The last three days seem so unreal to me. It's almost as if I organized this trip in my sleep – or rather, it organized itself. And now here I am, on Kurdish soil. I plant my foot firmly on the ground: no, I'm not dreaming.

By now it's four in the morning, and I am still pacing up and down in front of the airport building in Erbil with my Iraqi friend. Yousif lights a cigarette and sighs. I try to read his broad features, wondering what might be going through his mind. Two years ago he fled Iraq to escape death; today he is returning to pay his last respects to a dead father.

We stand waiting, staring into the distance, where the occasional flash of headlights can be seen. A taxi screeches to a halt beside us and picks up two men who were on the same plane as us. Now Yousif and I are the only ones left outside the sleepy provincial airport. The large parking lot opposite is gapingly empty.

At last, another pair of lights comes speeding toward us. An ancient Opel Astra brakes sharply and stops at the curbside directly in front of us. A well-built, slightly stocky man with fuzzy hair gets out. It is Basman, Yousif's brother. Yousif runs toward him and folds him wordlessly in his muscular arms. Then they release each other, still without speaking. After all, what is there to say, when there's so much that can't be put into words: fear and impotence, escape and displacement, the loss of your father and your family home?

I throw my small knapsack in the trunk, and now Basman greets me too, with a firm handshake. We pass a checkpoint where some heavily armed young men in uniform are hanging around. They wave us through with a weary gesture. Two more checkpoints and we are in Ankawa, a suburb of Erbil inhabited mainly by Christians. Here in the Kurdish autonomous region, Christians live in relative security, for the time being at least. We turn into a

dimly lit street leading to a housing development with rows
of identical-looking houses.

The car stops in front of a wall bearing a large black
placard. In the center is a luminous white cross, surrounded
by curly Arabic writing, also in white. "My father's death
notice," Yousif explains.

We clatter up a rusty iron staircase to the second
floor, and there on the mezzanine, at half past four in the
morning, stands Yousif's mother, Taghrid. She breaks
into loud sobs, and they hold each other fast. What a
reunion – their first glimpse of one another since Yousif's
perilous escape into the unknown two years ago! Only
this time, his father is absent. A reunion not in their home
country, but in exile; not in familiar surroundings, but in a
strange city; not in their spacious family home, but in a tiny
rented apartment.

Yousif was raised in Mosul. His father, Abu Yousif, had done
fairly well for himself, thanks to the family locksmith business. They owned a large house with a garden, where Abu
Yousif, whose illness confined him to a wheelchair for many
years, liked to sit. But then, a year and a half ago, Mosul was
occupied by the Islamic State. Yousif and his relatives are
Christians, and there is no place for Christians under IS's
black banner.

They had no choice but to flee with just the bare neces-
sities. Since then, the family has lived in this overcrowded
lodging in Erbil.

The walls look bare and forlorn, apart from some rosary
beads hung between two nails on one of them. We sit on
sofas. On a small table is a black-edged photo of Yousif's
father, a man with snow-white hair and eyes set deep in a
thin face already marked by his illness. Next to the photos
stands a shiny silver cross.

Taghrid wears widow's weeds, the uniform black relieved only by a few white wisps among her unkempt, shoulder-length hair. Her wrinkled face looks tired – very tired – despite having brightened a little at Yousif's arrival. Taghrid knocks on a thin wall; shortly afterward an uncle and aunt appear from next door with their two girls. Janet and Wasan have eyes like black pearls and look about fourteen and sixteen. They too are refugees from Mosul.

A nighttime reunion ensues, joy and pain mingling into one. We drink hot tea. Then the sofas are converted into beds; I am assigned a couch in the hall. Alone, I turn off the light and close my eyes. But I'm far too wound up to fall asleep. There's too much going around in my head. Finding myself here in northern Iraq for Abu Yousif's funeral still seems so unreal. Images float before my mind's eye. How did it all start? How did I get involved with Yousif and the other Iraqi and Syrian refugees in the first place?

....

Islam is a religion which arose on the Arabian Peninsula in the seventh century AD. It is based on the Koran, a religious text which, according to Islamic tradition, was revealed to the "divine messenger" Muhammad (570–632) and is held to be the direct word of God. The second main source of Islam is the Sunna (meaning "habitual practice"). This consists of the Prophet Muhammad's collected actions and sayings (hadith) and serves as a model for believers to follow.

Islam aspires to regulate every aspect of Muslim society, prescribing "five pillars" for a religious way of life: the testimony of faith, prayer, almsgiving, fasting in the month of Ramadan, and a pilgrimage to Mecca once in a lifetime.

Within Islam, a variety of currents and schools of thought have evolved. The Islamic State's professed goal is to restore the "original" Islamic faith.

....

2

Please Help Us!

When I first see the little boy – he looks about eleven – he catches my attention immediately. There is a hint of sadness in his big dark eyes. Though glimpsed only briefly, his image stays with me as I set about arranging jugs of water and apple juice on the table. Nearly forty people have responded to the invitation by our community to today's commemoration of Charles de Foucauld.

Charles de Foucauld was born in 1858, the son of a wealthy aristocratic family in Strasbourg, France. Having lost his Christian faith as a teenager, he made a career for himself in the army and became famous for his geographical explorations of Morocco. Through his encounters with Islam, he came to rethink his attitude toward God and rediscovered his Christian faith. He sought to imitate the life of Jesus in Nazareth, living by his own labor in simple surroundings. He joined a Trappist monastery in Syria, and later went to live as a hermit in the middle of the Sahara, where he befriended the nomadic tribes of Bedouin Muslims known as the Tuaregs. He shared in their lives, valued their culture, and strove for a dialogue with Islam.

Charles de Foucauld was shot on December 1, 1916, amid the turmoil of the First World War.

My community, the Little Brothers of Jesus, traces its origins back to this adventurer turned desert monk. Four of us have shared a house in a prefab housing project on the outskirts of Leipzig for the past ten years, and every year we invite friends and members of our parish to our ceremony on the first Sunday of Advent. When we were searching for a theme for our 2014 event, my fellow brother, Gianluca, had a brilliant idea: "Charles de Foucauld spent six years living as a monk in Syria. I have a Syrian colleague who's lived in Leipzig for years and is a Christian. He could tell us about the situation of Christians in Syria." We liked the idea and Gabriel and his family were duly invited.

As our little gathering gets under way, we are astonished to see more new faces in the room. Gabriel has interpreted our invitation very freely and brought a number of refugees from Syria and Iraq along with him. Most of them are clearly recent arrivals to our district, where there are still empty apartments in the prefabs from the old communist days. And now, sitting here at our tables, are women and men with jet-black hair and dark eyes, speaking a language I don't understand. The little boy belongs to this group too; he seems to have come with his father.

After the welcoming address, Gabriel steps up and begins to speak about his home city of Aleppo. We listen intently to his descriptions – delivered with characteristic Middle Eastern flourishes – of the ancient city with its famous citadel, a UNESCO World Heritage site. Leipzig is proud to be celebrating its thousandth anniversary in 2015. But what are a thousand years compared with the age-old cities of the Middle East, the cradle of civilization? Aleppo can look back over seven thousand years of history! And yet the war between cultures and nations is older still. Such a war is raging even now in Aleppo, Gabriel tells us. In the fight against opposition militias, helicopters sent by Syria's Assad regime are dropping barrel bombs and ripping out whole blocks of houses. Nearly two thousand of these iron barrels packed with explosive and bits of metal have been dropped on Aleppo. And Islamic State terrorists are shelling the Christian district bisected by the front between the deadly enemies.

"We Christians – as so often in my country's history – are caught in the crossfire. We are completely at the mercy of the terrorists. My brother-in-law was killed when IS militias bombarded our street again a few months ago. My sister is still living in Aleppo with four small children. She and her husband didn't want to leave their home, but now that she's a widow she doesn't have much choice. Only how can she get to Europe with four children?"

We are shocked to hear about the scale of the destruction and the cruelty inflicted. Our yearly commemoration is taking on a very somber tone. We've all been following the news about the war in Syria. But it's quite another thing to come face to face with Syrians who have fled the terror and seen their own family members killed. We are no longer talking anonymous statistics but faces: prematurely aged faces with immense suffering written in them. Faces still haunted by fear.

The dark brown eyes of that little boy. As the guests are dispersing and we start to wash the dishes, a thickset man of about forty comes up to me. He only speaks a few words of German. Beside him is the boy with the jet-black hair. Yousif – as the broad-shouldered stranger turns out to be called – addresses me. I don't understand, but the boy already speaks excellent German and translates for him, "We are from Iraq, from Mosul. Please help us!"

I suddenly feel giddy as the multitude of tasks awaiting me flashes before my eyes: my duties at the prison and in the parish always pile up in the weeks before Christmas. The student Catholic society is offering a four-week course entitled "Spiritual Exercises in Everyday Life," and I have promised to run eight counseling sessions each week. All this and much more weighs on my mind. I feel like saying, "Sorry, . . . I'd love to . . . but I haven't got time."

But I can't do it. The young boy's look melts my heart. I can't say no. I ask, "Don't you have anyone to support you?" The boy translates my question for his father, who shakes his head. "Can you give me your phone number?" Amanuel, as the boy is called, writes down a cell phone number on a paper napkin. The next day, I call to arrange a visit. My life hasn't been the same since.

A few days later, I ring the doorbell of an eleven-story apartment block in the Miltitzer Allee. Yousif lives on the third floor with his wife, Tara, and their two children, Amanuel and Shaba. They invite me into their living room. The walls are adorned with religious images: a rather gaudy painting of the Last Supper and a portrait of Saint George, alongside a calendar in Arabic with a photo of a bearded bishop.

Yousif's request for help, I learn, concerns his children. There are problems at school. Amanuel, a handsome, slightly built boy, confides to me that he is regularly bullied by his Muslim schoolmates because of the small cross he wears around his neck. Amanuel has always worn this cross, even when things got dangerous for Christians in Mosul. I promise to get in touch with the principal. Then I ask Yousif – with Amanuel's help – to tell me something of their story.

In Mosul, Tara and Yousif had been very involved in the
Syrian Orthodox Church. But after 2003, everything
changed.

The United States and Britain attacked Iraq on the
premise that the country had developed weapons of mass
destruction. Subsequent investigations revealed this to be
merely a pretext. While, on the face of it, the war may have
been about the removal of the dictator Saddam Hussein and
the "import" of democracy, the subtext was undoubtedly
the export of cheap oil.

In response to the American-led invasion of Iraq, Muslim
clerics called for a holy war. Large numbers of fundamentalist jihadists from all over the Islamic world came together
to wage war on the "unbelievers." Christians in Iraq became
fair game for the Islamists.

But why were local Christians singled out as prime
targets for their attacks? The fact that the Prophet
Muhammad was both a religious and political leader
means that religion and politics have always been closely
interwoven in Islam: consequently, war can also take on a
religious dimension. In the eyes of many Muslims, Western
nations are "Christian" states. Therefore, in the event of
attack by those states, Christians in the Middle East are
suspected of being collaborators and allies of the invaders.
The Christians' precarious situation was worsened by a
speech by President George W. Bush, in which he called his
war a "crusade," thereby stirring up deep-seated Muslim
resentment against the West. The Iraqi Christians, who had
never been involved in a crusade in their two-thousand-year
history, were seen as guilty by association and subjected
to a regime of terror. They became scapegoats on whom
revenge could be exacted for the aggression of the "Christian occupiers."

For example, protection money was extorted from Christians by invoking the ancient Islamic practice of levying a special tax, referred to as *jizya* in the Koran, on non-Muslims. Under Islamic (shari'a) law, Christians must pay *jizya* for the privilege of being allowed – albeit to a very limited extent – to practice their religion.

According to Yousif, the sums demanded increased year by year. You paid up because you knew what the alternative would be: destruction of your property, and murder. Even Christian churches became targets of the terror perpetrated in the name of Islam. Yet many Christians still wouldn't contemplate leaving Mosul, cherishing the faint hope that the nightmare would come to an end one day. Among these were Yousif and Tara.

. . . .

The **Koran** is the holy book of Islam and is believed by Muslims to contain the Word of God as revealed to the Prophet Muhammad through the angel Gabriel over the course of twenty-two years.

The early revelations (in Mecca) are characterized by openness and tolerance. They reflect the situation of the prophet who, despite his lack of political power, attempted to win over the people of Mecca, as well as Jews and Christians, to the new religion. The later revelations (in Medina) are quite different: by this time, Muhammad had achieved political and military power, and was both a religious leader and statesman.

The Koran consists of 114 suras (chapters) which are organized not chronologically but roughly in order of length. Where contradictions occur, the prevailing Islamic doctrine teaches that the newer (later) verses are to be seen as correcting or superseding the older ones.

Accordingly, many Koranic scholars argue that the newer verses calling for war on non-Muslims override all the other verses exhorting to peaceable conduct.

. . . .

Instead, things got even worse. One day, an anonymous caller threatened to cut off Yousif's left arm. He knew immediately what the caller was getting at, as he had a large cross tattooed on his brawny left forearm. "You just try!" Yousif retorted impulsively, and hung up.

It was plain to him that he was living dangerously now. And that his young family was at risk too. A few days later, the phone rang again: "If you're not gone in three days, you will go to hell!" Yousif knew he had to act fast, and left Mosul with his wife and their two children. They made for Erbil, the capital of the Kurdish autonomous region in northern Iraq. There he was safe, but unable to find work. After much agonizing, he made up his mind to flee to Europe, preferably to Germany or Sweden.

This journey had to be undertaken alone. Though it broke Yousif's heart to leave them behind, such a venture was far too hazardous for his wife and children, the only route being via the dark machinations of a people-smuggling gang. The price demanded was seventeen thousand US dollars. Yousif sold everything he possibly could and borrowed the rest from friends and relatives. Even now, he tells me, he still owes five thousand.

The smugglers took him over the Turkish border. He wasn't allowed to take any luggage with him, and had to surrender his passport. There were days of waiting around. Then he was taken in a car to another town and, with just the clothes on his back, crammed into a hidden compartment inside a semitrailer. It was a large truck transporting vegetables across the Bosporus, Greece, and the Balkans to Germany.

Inside the trailer, a double wall was fitted directly behind the tractor unit. The entrance was inside the trailer, via a trapdoor in the rear wall that was so well concealed as to be invisible. Yousif squeezed through this opening into a dark space so narrow he could only stand up by leaning sideways to accommodate his broad shoulders. On the floor was some corrugated foam rubber for sitting or lying on. A few plastic water bottles and packets of cookies were piled up in a corner; no other food was provided. There were two palm-sized air holes to prevent the occupant from suffocating and through which he could relieve himself, though only while the vehicle was in motion; whenever it stopped, absolute silence had to be maintained.

Yousif's heart beat wildly as the trapdoor was screwed tight from the outside, leaving him incarcerated in his dark dungeon. The truck set off and later he could hear some men loading the trailer. Seven days and seven nights Yousif spent in this cramped, lightless space. Sometimes he would fall asleep from sheer exhaustion, but even in his sleep he was tortured by fear: what if he suffocated inside this cage? What if he was discovered during border checks? And could he trust the smugglers, who had made him hand over the full payment in advance? Might they release him from his cell on some lonely back road only to kill him? But worst of all was the bitter anguish he felt at the thought of the wife and children he had left behind.

There was one point where it all nearly went wrong. The truck had been stationary for some time and Yousif was fighting to stay awake. He knew that he snored, and that the noise could prove his downfall. Suddenly he started. Someone was tapping the outer wall with a metal object. Had his snoring betrayed him? Were they checking the truck for a hidden cavity? Yousif's heart was in his mouth, and he hardly dared to breathe. Outside, loud voices were arguing in a foreign language. Then the engine started up.

Breathing a sigh of relief, Yousif slumped to the floor and
fell fast asleep.

Finally, after seven days of darkness, he heard the trailer
being unloaded; then the truck rumbled off again. A couple
of hours later, it stopped. The trapdoor was unscrewed and
opened; Yousif crawled out and was helped down by the
driver. His limbs were stiff and he could hardly walk. He
rubbed his eyes, now unaccustomed to the light. He was in
an empty parking lot, lit feebly by a couple of streetlamps. It
was bitterly cold and there wasn't a sound to be heard apart
from the rumble of the engine.

The driver pointed in the direction of the local station.
There Yousif was to wait for a man who would return his
passport.

"How will I recognize him?" Yousif asked.

"He'll recognize you – he has your passport photo."

The driver climbed hurriedly back into his cab and
stepped on the gas. Yousif stood uncertainly for a few
moments in the deserted parking lot. Then, pulling himself
together, he stumbled on his way, still feeling very stiff.
Soon, he was hiking along the road in the indicated direction, speeding up a little with each step. Spotting a white
license plate in unfamiliar lettering on a passing vehicle, he
read: C – Chemnitz. He was in Germany.

For four hours Yousif waited outside Chemnitz station
for the stranger who was supposed to return his passport. A
red neon sign showed minus twenty degrees Celsius (minus
four Fahrenheit). He was shaking all over with cold. Nobody
came. By now, day was breaking and Yousif stopped a pass-
erby: "Police?" At the police station, they wanted to see his
papers. Yousif couldn't make himself understood. One of
the police officers saw the leaden fatigue in Yousif's face and
offered him a comfortable chair. He sat down and fell asleep

on the spot. An hour later he was awoken and, with the aid of an interpreter, related his story.

Afterwards, he was taken to a hostel for asylum seekers, where he was able to talk to his wife and parents on the phone for the first time in four weeks. At last, a sign of life after four weeks that felt like an eternity!

For another six months, Yousif lived in an agony of uncertainty: Would things remain calm in Ankawa? Was there a chance that Tara and the children might be able to come to Germany soon? Would his parents – left behind in Mosul – be put under pressure or even murdered by the jihadists? Such thoughts and fears tortured him night and day. And he felt so helpless in this new country, whose language he didn't understand and whose bureaucracy was a mystery to him. Finally, his asylum application was accepted and he was able to bring Tara over with Amanuel and Shaba by legal means. What a reunion it was at the Berlin airport after those long, anxious months!

At the same time, his home city of Mosul was occupied by IS militias, forcing his parents, his brother, and all his relatives, along with the entire Christian community, to leave the city and flee to Ankawa.

3

A Graveside Reunion

My head is still buzzing with memories of my first
encounter with Yousif, mixed with impressions from this,
our spontaneous trip to Ankawa. It's hard to believe I am
actually here in Kurdistan, staying with Yousif's family.
I turn over, in the hope of dropping off to sleep at last.
Outside, day is already breaking.

Two hours later, I am woken by the clatter of dishes in
the next room and get up quickly. Taghrid, Yousif, and
Basman are already sitting on one of the sofas, bent over a
low table laid with tea cups, flatbreads, and a bowl of yogurt.
"Marhaba," I greet them, followed by a few words of English.
I sit down next to Yousif.

"Did you sleep well?" I ask.

Yousif shakes his head.

"I wanted to see my father, but not in the cemetery."

I put a hand on his shoulder.

"Has he been buried already?"

"Here the dead are always buried immediately."

"And the ceremony today?"

"That will take place in the church. There will be a special
prayer for my father at the Sunday service, then we'll go to
the cemetery."

As we leave the apartment, Yousif's mother warns me not
to leave any valuables behind. "Ali Baba!" she says, pointing

to my knapsack. I get the message and take my papers and airline ticket with me.

We bump along the potholed roads of Ankawa in Basman's worn-out old car. There are neither trees nor bushes in this desert-like country; the only things shooting out of the ground here are concrete buildings. The building sites all look dilapidated. Yousif explains that Kurdistan had initially seen a construction boom: oil production brought money into the country, and with it foreign companies with a skilled labor force. Meanwhile, refugees from other regions of Iraq – including Christians – have been pouring into Kurdistan for years, attracted by its relative political and economic stability. But over the last year or so, due to the collapse of oil prices on the world market, nearly all the building projects have been abandoned and the government has run out of money.

It's certainly not an attractive sight: concrete pillars sticking up into the rainy, gray sky, surrounded by piles of debris and rusty iron grids. And the picture is made bleaker still by the garbage along the roads. Plastic bags shredded by the wind hang from the few thorny bushes: bizarre Christmas tree decorations, or perhaps a mirror image of the people here; ejected from their homes and left to the mercy of the four winds, they too are caught in a barren, desolate landscape.

A large road sign indicates the way to Mosul in Arabic and Latin script.

"Your home, Yousif!" I shout from the back.

"It *was* my home once," Yousif replies from the passenger seat, and I can hear the sadness in his voice.

We arrive at a large, ugly building and Basman looks around for a parking space.

"This is our church."

Despite my reputedly vivid imagination, I cannot begin
to guess the original purpose of this austere, makeshift
place of worship, which is now filling up with people
dressed in black. On the end wall is a cross, and beneath
it an altar bearing a shiny chalice and candlesticks. A
drawn-back red curtain gives the slightly raised chancel the
appearance of a stage. Below it are around three hundred
chairs, most of which are already occupied. I follow Yousif's
family to the front and sit in the first row. I am struck by
the gravity of the women's and men's faces – framed by
grief like a black-edged envelope. Some of them are bent
over, as if crushed by fate, hard work, the death of a friend.
Yousif's unexpected presence comes as a great surprise
to this grieving, exiled community. Stony faces brighten
with smiles and a few people come forward to embrace the
returnee. An extraordinary reunion in a setting at once
strange and familiar.

Gradually, things get underway in the chancel. Several
men in white robes move to and fro with books or candles
and begin to sing. The melody sounds alien to my ears:
full-throated and Eastern, with a mournful tone. A young,
black-bearded man in a bright red robe solemnly swings
a censer, setting twelve gold bells jingling and sending up
a cloud of incense that fills the room with its heady scent.
Other men in colorful robes appear, presumably priests
or deacons. At the side of the chancel is a red upholstered
chair occupied by an old man with a silver-grey beard. He
wears a black habit and a round, red cap.

"That's Bishop Saliba, the old Bishop of Mosul – he lives
in exile here," Yousif whispers to me.

The enchantingly beautiful singing flows back and forth
in waves between the men in the chancel and the congregation. The women – as I have only just noticed – have covered
their hair with scarves: fine, almost transparent silk scarves,

some black, some white, some patterned. We stand for
most of the service. The Bible is placed center stage on the
lectern; the liturgy is conducted in Syriac.

Why Syriac, I wonder – aren't we in Iraq? And what
exactly is Syriac anyway? It can't be the national language of
Syria – that's Arabic.

I remember asking Yousif where he was from right at the
beginning of our friendship. He said Mosul and searched
on his smartphone for a translation of the Arabic word
"Suryani": Syrian.

"What – you mean you're Syrian?" I asked, utterly
confused. Yousif began to explain.

Many people associate the word "Syrian" with the state
of Syria. But the Syrian Arab Republic has only existed since
1944 and is a product of European colonialism: after the
First World War, parts of the Ottoman Empire were placed
under the control of the victorious powers, Britain and
France. The borders, drawn with a ruler and without regard
for ethnic or religious groups, demarcated the new states of
Iraq and Syria.

After searching some more on his smartphone, Yousif
showed me another word: "Aramean." I recognized it from
the Bible, where an ancient creed recalls, "A wandering
Aramean was my father" (Deut. 26:5).

I listen closely to the singing in the Aramaic language
and especially to the words of the Gospel as Jesus would
have spoken them. In his day, Hebrew was only retained as
the language of the Bible and the liturgy; the ordinary folk
spoke Aramaic. In other words, if Jesus had preached in
Damascus, Aleppo, or Antioch, he would have been understood there too.

Yousif, like most Christians from Mosul, speaks Arabic.
But the Christians who were driven out of the villages of
the Nineveh Plains, not far from Mosul, still speak Aramaic

to this day. Whether the language has a future is doubtful, however.

I am particularly moved by the Lord's Prayer, whose petitions are sung with outstretched arms, by men and women in turn. The alternating chant is beautiful: loud, fervent, and poignant. The people sing with heart and soul about the Passion of Christ, and the words resonate with their own sufferings. I feel a shiver run down my spine: I am listening to the songs of a suffering people, perhaps even the requiem of a dying church. Are these the last Christians, singing their last song with their last breath? I close my eyes and am transported by the plaintive Eastern melodies.

. . . .

The **Arameans**, sometimes also known as Assyrians or Syrians, were among the original inhabitants of a large area encompassing eastern Turkey along with northern Iraq and Syria, as distinct from the Muslim Arab tribes who have held sway there since the seventh century AD. This ethnic group descended from the Assyrians, Chaldeans, and Arameans who settled in Syria and Mesopotamia thousands of years ago.

Ancient Syria is also the birthplace of the first Christian churches. The apostle Paul was baptized in Damascus, while Peter is said to have been the first bishop of Antioch (now Turkish Antakya). The "Syriac" Christians can trace their roots directly back to the early church, from which several lines evolved, such as the Syriac Orthodox Church. Once again, the name has nothing to do with the modern state of Syria and, in view of the elusive nature of the term "Syrian," the Syriac Christians are generally referred to in the following as Aramaic Christians.

In the early days of Christianity, the Bible was translated into Aramaic in the Syrian cultural area and the liturgy was celebrated in the same tongue, which developed into an important literary language and was usually referred to as "Syriac." (In fact, the word "Syrian" eventually became a synonym for "Christian.") Syriac/Aramaic was still widely spoken up to the time of the

Crusades, after which it was gradually displaced by Arabic. Today, only a minority of Syriac Christians are native Aramaic speakers, although the liturgy is still celebrated in this ancient Semitic language even today.

A hand on my arm brings me back to earth. Yousif is nudging me to pass on the sign of peace. This ritual gesture begins with the priest, or rather with Christ, at the altar. With his left hand on the altar, the priest turns to the congregation and extends his right arm toward them with the words, "Peace and comfort be with you all!"

Then the deacon passes the peace to the people: a man dressed in white approaches the front row and places both hands around the joined hands of the first person, who turns to his neighbor and passes on the greeting likewise.

To me, the liturgy has a mixture of strangeness and familiarity about it. I can't understand the words but can guess the contents of the rites and prayers. Finally, bread and wine are distributed and we celebrate communion – irrespective of language and church affiliation.

After the service we get back into Basman's rust-nibbled car, and he drives us to the cemetery at breakneck speed. "At this rate I'll be going to my own funeral," I think to myself. Even Yousif comments, "After two years of living in Germany, I don't think I could ever drive here again."

The Mosul Christian migrants have established their own cemetery in Ankawa. At the entrance is a gate with a cross, and beyond it are long rows of graves with small, whitish headstones of identical format. Each stone bears the same emblem: a cross in the top center framed by two olive branches, signifying "through Christ to peace." The place reminds me of a war cemetery. I guess there must be about a thousand graves here, occupied by exiled Mosul Christians awaiting a new – and permanent – resting place.

I am told mortality is unusually high here. And it's not just due to hygiene problems and lack of medical care, either – there are emotional factors at play too. After all, what is there left to live for when you've lost everything and no longer have a future anywhere? This cemetery is fast becoming the epilogue of a dying community: Will there eventually be nothing left of the Eastern Orthodox churches but a burial ground, soon to be overgrown with the grass of neglect? Everywhere I look it's the same: the women at the graveside are dressed in the trademark color of death and mourning. Even the sky above us is wearing black. A storm is brewing, and throbbing military helicopters circle beneath the low-hanging clouds – a reminder that the IS front isn't far away – and that its mission is "subjugation."

At Abu Yousif's grave, prayers are spoken in Aramaic. The headstone isn't in place yet – just a couple of thin blue candles stuck in the freshly turned brown earth. Next to us, a long row of open graves await their dead. I pluck up courage and sing a German song: "O Jesus, you are my whole life – without you, only death!" We stand in silence for a while, then we drive – at far too lively a pace for the bumpy road – back to the building where Yousif's family has found temporary accommodation.

4.

Last Respects

In Ankawa, whole rows of hastily erected two-story buildings are rented out at a premium to families from Mosul.
Yousif's mother has him translate for me, "Our kitchen in
Mosul was bigger than these two rooms put together. But
we still struggle to pay the rent, because only Basman has
found a job. And a poorly paid one at that." Taghrid is glad
for the bit of money Yousif manages to send home every
now and again. Only families with relatives in America or
Europe who are able to support them can afford even such
a primitive lodging as this; the only other alternative is the
refugee camp.

In each of the two ground floor rooms occupied by other
members of Yousif's family, a large circle of chairs has been
arranged around the blank walls, and the photo of Yousif's
father placed on a low coffee table beside a small standing
cross and a miniature incense holder. Out of respect for
the Muslim guests expected among the party, one of the
rooms has been assigned to men and the other to women.
Wadid, one of the deceased's brothers, sprinkles incense
on the glowing coals at regular intervals, giving the place
a strong church smell. I sit down on one of the chairs. Our
bare room quickly fills up with relatives and acquaintances
and – judging by the babble of women's voices – so does the

one next door. Outside, raindrops are drumming on the
plastic roofing.

Whenever a new person arrives, the room falls silent and
everyone gets up. The newcomer murmurs a prayer, while
the other guests mouth the words with outstretched hands.
Then we sit down again and talk among ourselves – until the
next visitor arrives. The older men finger their worry beads,
the young ones their phones.

I am sitting next to Wadid, who introduces himself as an
uncle of Yousif. He used to work with Yousif's father in the
family locksmith business. Wadid speaks a little English,
and Yousif helps us out here and there, translating from
Arabic into German. I marvel at how quickly Yousif has
mastered German, given that it was less than a year ago
when we first met, and that, back then, he had needed his
son Amanuel to interpret. I admire the energy that Yousif
and many other refugees devote to learning our cumber-
some language. For starters, it means reading and writing
in a completely opposite direction. Many of the refugees I
know are the same age as me or older. I can't begin to think
how I would manage if I were driven out of Germany and
granted asylum in, say, Saudi Arabia. I wouldn't even be able
to read the street names. Would I have the perseverance
to learn a whole new alphabet and language? And how far
would I get with it?

As a craftsman, Yousif never had any reason to learn
other languages. Yet in the space of a year, he has acquired
such an excellent command of German that he can translate
for me with ease.

At this point, thick coffee is served Arab-style in tiny
cups, spiced with cardamom. The first guests get up to go,
and others enter. A quiet, reverent coming and going.

I sit in a corner with Wadid and Yousif, chatting in hushed tones about the history of their family and the fate of Mosul.

Mosul lies on the Tigris, across the river from the ruined biblical city of Nineveh. With a population of two million, Mosul is the second-largest city in Iraq, and was regarded as a center of Eastern Christianity due to its large number of Christian inhabitants, churches, and monasteries. Of the 1.4 million Christians still living in Iraq around 1990, there were two hundred thousand in Mosul alone. At that time there were still five hundred churches in Iraq where services were held on a regular basis.

Before the rise of the Islamic State, Christians had already been emigrating for years due to the war and the desperate economic situation. Increasing numbers of often well-educated indigenous Christians opted to leave the country where their families and their faith had been rooted for nearly two thousand years. On top of this came the growing pressure exerted by radical Islamic groups ("Salafists"). Al-Qaeda (meaning base or foundation) had been set up in 1993 as a loose network of Islamist organizations in order to create a solid "base" for the propagation of Islam.

When the Americans invaded Iraq in 2003, there were seventy thousand Christians left in Mosul. From then on, Wadid tells me, the long-established Iraqi Christians – as alleged allies of the (Christian) United States – came under even heavier fire from the Islamists.

....

The term **Salafism** (from *salaf*, meaning "ancestors") is used to characterize ultraconservative movements that hark back to the early days of Islam. They are literally "fundamentalist," in that they advocate a return to the foundations of the faith. As such, they insist on a literal reading of the Koran and strict emulation of the Prophet Muhammad according to the Sunna (tradition). Salafism is currently the fastest-growing radical movement within Islam. Part of the Salafist movement seeks to attain power by legal means. Another faction takes a militant approach, justifying violence as a legitimate instrument of jihad (holy war), hence the use of the term jihadists or mujahideen (jihad warriors) to describe its followers.

The **Wahhabis** (named after the eighteenth-century preacher Abd al-Wahhab) regard themselves as Salafists whose mission is to restore the original values of Islam. Adherents of all other interpretations of the Koran, and all non-Muslims in particular, are declared "unbelievers" and their right to life is denied based on a Salafist reading of the text. According to al-Wahhab's personal recommendation, all those who refuse to subscribe to his doctrine should have their property confiscated and their wives and daughters should be violated. Wahhabism is the official Islamic doctrine of Saudi Arabia. The Al-Qaeda network and the Islamic State are ideologically very close to Wahhabism.

Islamism is a modern political ideology which seeks to establish an Islamic state modeled on the "original Muslim community" and justifies the use of violence to that end on religious grounds. Since religion and politics have always been intertwined in Islam, it is impossible to separate Islamism from Islam by arguing that the former has nothing to do with the latter: Islamists profess to practice "true Islam" and support their claim by referencing specific doctrines and authorities from Islam's history.

The term "Islamism" is also problematic in the sense that no such differentiation exists in any other religion. Violent movements within the Christian church (such as the Crusades, for example) are laid squarely at the door of Christianity, and not distinguished from "true Christianity" as "Christianist."

Where the term "Islamist" is used here notwithstanding, it is generally to draw attention to the existence of "Islamism" as a

violent political and ideological current within Islam as distinct
from many other schools of thought (e.g., the nonviolent Muslim
Reform movement).

....

Al-Qaeda boomed in Mosul as elsewhere, and one of the
city's monasteries became the target of a rocket attack in
the same year. The following year, Saint Paul's Cathedral
in Mosul was badly destroyed by a bomb. Attacks on
churches and churchgoers multiplied: a five-year-old
boy and his slightly older sister were shot on their way to
Mass, Christian girls were raped for not wearing a veil,
and death threats – whether via text or pamphlets through
the door – were a daily occurrence. Christian schools
were threatened with bomb attacks; unless the students
converted to Islam, their lives would no longer be secure.

Wadid recalls with horror how Islamist militias in Mosul
began to stop passersby in the street and demand to see
their passports. Because Iraqi passports include the bearer's
religion, anyone thus identified as a Christian lived in fear
of being murdered. They had heard the story of Ayad Tariq,
a fourteen-year-old Assyrian Christian boy in Baqubah,
Iraq, who had been interrogated by the "religious fighters,"
as they call themselves.

"Allahu akbar! God is great!" they cried. "You are a Christian, an unbeliever."

"I am a Christian, but not an unbeliever," the boy replied.

Ayad got no further – the Islamists seized him and
hacked off his head.

Moreover, it was the Mosul Christians, many of whom
were educated and from a well-to-do background, who
were largely made to foot the bill for the terror, through

protection rackets or ransoms for abducted family
members.

Uncle Wadid relates in a near-whisper how masked,
armed men appeared one day in the office of their small
family business and took away the laptops, expressly to
help organize their terror regime. In this way, he tells us,
Al-Qaeda went about building up an insidious industry of
kidnapping and extortion using mafia-like intelligence.

I try to imagine what everyday life must have been like
in such a climate. "So what was your relationship like with
neighbors and business colleagues – some of them must
have been Muslims too?"

"We had good neighborly relations, or at least we thought
so. But then our city became more and more Islamic."

"How do you mean?"

"More and more women started to wear headscarves,
and men began to grow long beards. Children were taught
at school to think of Christians as impure, so that Muslim
children would no longer play with our girls and boys. For
us parents, it was terrible to see our children being progres-
sively pushed aside; whether at school or in the street, they
were constantly made to feel inferior. On top of that came
the fear they might be kidnapped or murdered."

Yousif also remembers: "Those Friday sermons in the
mosques – we couldn't avoid hearing them over the loudspeakers from the minarets. It made me sick to the stomach
to hear the imams stirring up hatred against Christians,
and calling on their followers to kill unbelievers in the name
of the Koran. They even used to pray, 'Allah, bless us and kill
the unbelievers.'"

I hear one horror story after another. In 2006, the Syrian
Orthodox priest responsible for the community to which
Yousif's family belonged – the church of Mar Aphrem – was

abducted by Muslim extremists. The condition of his release was that the church should disown a speech given by Pope Benedict XVI in Regensburg, Germany. In a lecture at the university there, the pope had quoted the words of a Byzantine emperor to a Muslim: "Show me just what Muhammad brought that was new, and there you will find things only evil and inhuman, such as his command to spread by the sword the faith he preached."

The relatives of Abuna (Father) Paulos Iskandar duly distanced themselves from the pope's words and paid the ransom demanded – yet the priest's arms and legs were still cut off. And all to avenge the Prophet Muhammad for the outrageous criticism that he used violence to spread religion!

Whatever the cause – a papal address in Germany, a threatened burning of the Koran by the evangelical pastor Terry Jones in the United States, a Muhammad caricature in Denmark – Iraqi Christians are invariably made to pay the price, and with their own blood.

In 2007, Muslim extremists killed Abuna Raghild along with three deacons and blew up the corpses so that nothing but shreds were left – a reflection of just how deep the hatred went. Christians were not even worthy of a burial; the killers would rather leave their remains for dogs to scavenge.

In 2008, Bishop Paulos Faraj Rahho was abducted. The aim was to force the church to supply Christian suicide bombers to inflict terror on the Kurdish autonomous region and so extort the release of jihadists detained there. Because his church rejected violence on principle, he was murdered. His body was found on a trash dump – yet another instance of the contempt felt by radical Muslims toward people of other faiths. To them, Christians were just garbage.

Sitting here surrounded by people from Mosul, I am
appalled by the atrocities they have suffered. I wonder
whether I haven't been paying enough attention to the
persecution of Iraqi Christians in the news. Or do such
stories simply vanish too quickly from the radar of our
Western media? The unfortunate law of habituation dictates
that when terror attacks are carried out with such brutal
regularity, they become too routine to mention – and I,
like anyone else, am a consumer of *news*. In that sense,
the Mosul Christians share the fate of victims in many
of the world's trouble spots. Who spares a thought for
the murdered of El Salvador, the gang wars in Congo, the
torture victims in the prisons of many dictatorships, or the
attacks still being carried out in Baghdad?

Yousif draws an audible breath. "We Christians were
a sitting target for the Islamist militias and the mob.
The terror shaped our daily life – car bombs, abductions,
murder. We lived in fear, constantly wondering when it
would be our turn."

I'm finding it increasingly easy to understand why Yousif
fled after the jihadist's threat to cut off his arm. But what
a cruel decision to be faced with: to have to leave a parent
behind in a wheelchair in order to seek safety for yourself
and your wife and children! And how badly he had wanted
to see his father again! I glance at the photo and the cross
next to it, wondering what Yousif's father went through in
the last few months of his life. What was written in his sad,
solemn eyes?

I had read in a book on the Islamic State that some three
thousand IS fighters infiltrated the city of Mosul from
January to June 2014. They terrorized the inhabitants and
collected fifteen million dollars a month in protection
money, almost exclusively from Christians. There were

periodic killings of police officers or soldiers, and car bombs were an ever-present threat. The tension grew unbearable.

The IS strategy worked, leaving the military and police so intimidated and demoralized that it was an easy thing to take control of Mosul. In the night from June 9 to 10, 2014, the fate of Mosul Christians was sealed. The Iraqi army fled almost without a fight, leaving its modern Western weapons in the hands of the Islamic State. Once the jihadists had taken the city, things were relatively calm for a while. Perhaps the Islamic State wanted to secure its new sovereignty first, and fill all strategically important posts with its own people.

The **Islamic State** (known up to 2014 by its self-given name of "Islamic State in Iraq and Syria" or ISIS) represents an extreme, fundamentalist version of Islam which professes to follow the Koran and the example of the Prophet Muhammad to the letter. Its mobilizing power is derived partly from a promise to liberate Muslims from the political, economic, and ideological paternalism of the "Christian crusaders" (the Western states). In order to shake off once and for all the colonialism which it claims is responsible for the plight of the Arab states, it appeals to the Arab peoples' sense of offended honor by vowing to rise up and wreak revenge.

Social problems, high unemployment, and corrupt Arab elites have also served to boost the popularity of the Islamic State. The collapse of modern Arab states built on the Western model make the Islamic State's promised cure-all particularly credible and attractive: only a state founded on religion can guarantee justice and security, therefore Islam is the solution.

Jonah, another of Yousif's uncles, who has been listening in silence up to this point, draws his chair closer to us. To my astonishment, this quiet, introspective man addresses me in

German. I learn that Jonah lived in Leipzig for a year in 1977, and he still speaks pretty good German – with a touch of Saxon dialect. A book printer by trade, he came to Leipzig to gain a further qualification in printing press operation. This time, Yousif translates our German conversation into Arabic so that Wadid can follow it.

"After IS had taken Mosul, we heard a few days later on the radio that the new rulers were inviting us Christians to return to the city. We were promised we would be treated well, and were naïve enough to believe it. We *wanted* to believe it, because we longed to go back to our homes and our place of origin. We were also told there would be no more murders or car bombs. So we made our way back to Mosul. But it was a false peace. Days later a message boomed out of the mosque loudspeakers ordering us to convert to Islam or pay *jizya*."

On July 18, 2014, the self-appointed caliph of the Islamic State, the Islam scholar Abu Bakr al-Baghdadi, confronted Christians with this alternative, giving them twenty-four hours to comply with his ultimatum. Those who refused to yield to shari'a law would be punished by the sword.

"We knew what that meant," Wadid continues, "so we fled a second time. But all the roads leading out of the huge city were patrolled. We had to get out at a checkpoint and hand over everything we had loaded into our cars: cell phones, computers, money, jewelry. Even our wedding rings!" he adds, showing me his bare fingers.

"But we remained loyal," he smiles. "We never betrayed our faith."

I am moved by his words, and we are silent for a moment. An elderly man enters the room. We get up to pray.

When we are seated again, Wadid adds with quiet emotion, "And our houses in Mosul: they came and marked them out with spray cans." I had heard before about the spray-painting of Christian houses with a scarlet "nūn" – the Arabic letter "n," standing for "Nassarah" (Nazarenes), as Christians are referred to in the Koran.

"That meant the house had been confiscated for IS and declared free for looting," Jonah elaborates. "Even colleagues and neighbors we'd been on good terms with for decades refused to stand by us when IS invaded – it was heartbreaking."

Uncle Jonah looks at me with raised eyebrows, "You may not believe this, but a Muslim neighbor actually called me on my cell phone to boast that he had robbed my house and donated half the stolen property to IS."

I hear time and again of such bitterly disappointing betrayals of Christians by their Muslim neighbors. How could this happen? Had they been deceived all those years? Had the neighbors merely feigned friendship in order to profit from them? Or was the temptation of helping themselves to Christian property with impunity just too great? Were neighbors and friends afraid they might become a target for the IS terrorists themselves? No doubt all these factors could have played a role.

Admittedly, there were religious reasons too: relations between Christians and their Muslim neighbors were fine as long as religion wasn't the be-all and end-all. At least that's how Jonah interprets the change of mood: the more religious the Muslim environment became, the more intolerant or even hostile Muslims grew toward Christians. This assertion disturbs me, but I can't probe any further because Jonah has already risen to greet an acquaintance.

With each new guest who comes to pay their respects, I learn more about the fate of the Mosul Christians. Many owned their own homes; they had jobs, cars, friends,

hobbies . . . and all had to leave their home city purely
because of their faith. The man next to me tells me in good
English that he fled east from Mosul to the Christian town
of Qaraqosh, and from there to Erbil. Where else was left?

Jonah sighs, "We have lost everything. Even our history.
After nearly two thousand years, we have been uprooted.
Can such an old tree ever be transplanted?" He goes on to
relate how IS terrorists cut down and burned all the trees
in his family's garden in Mosul – a symbolic act by those
seeking the root-and-branch destruction of the Christian
population.

Yousif pulls out his smartphone and plays a couple of
videos of bearded terrorists tearing down crosses from
church domes and spires and hoisting the black banner
of IS. Masked men smashing statues of saints with huge
hammers and toppling a figure of the Virgin Mary from
its plinth to jubilant cries. Several churches such as
Mar Aphrem or Mar Yousif have since been turned into
mosques.

Another young man enters the room. We pray, and the
incense is refilled. I sit down next to him and he tells me in
fluent English that he managed to find a job in the oil fields
of Kurdistan, but lost it again when the oil price fell, leaving
him condemned to idleness, with no money and no future
prospects. In the midst of his tale, we are suddenly thrown
into darkness, as the storm outside has caused the power
to cut out. But people are used to regular outages here, and
cordless lamps are brought in, their cold, greenish light
casting a chill over the place. Outside, a generator springs
noisily into action, restoring power to the street after a few
minutes.

Later on, a lavish meal is served, beautifully presented
on a collection of platters. Prepared by Yousif's family and
relatives, the typical Mosul specialties are a feast for all the

senses. We dig in and the mood lightens, becoming almost cheery. I sample fried meatballs with rice, strips of meat in a hot spicy sauce, and colorful salads. The leftovers are traditionally shared among the needy, Yousif tells me.

The conflict between **Sunnis** and **Shiites** has been and remains the cause of numerous attacks and military confrontations, as the battle for supremacy between the two "Islamic superpowers" of Saudi Arabia (Sunni) and Iran (Shiite) is played out in countries such as Iraq, Yemen, and Syria.

Ever since the death of Muhammad, Islam has been split over the issue of who should carry forward the prophet's religious and political legacy. Shiites (meaning the "Party of Ali") assume that Muhammad appointed his cousin Ali as his rightful successor, while Sunnis regard the first caliphs as the prophet's legitimate heirs, based on a particular reading of the Sunna (the example set by the prophet).

The Sunni–Shiite conflict has always been a very bloody one. For centuries – right up to the present day – the dispute over the prophet's succession has been the source of a deadly enmity, which erupts periodically into acts of excessive violence.

Among the funeral party guests is a Muslim family. Omar, the husband, is a likeable man. His wife, unlike the Christian women, wears a headscarf. She goes next door with their two small children, while Omar comes and sits with us. And when the next Christian arrives and speaks the prayer for the deceased, he unhesitatingly rises, spreads his hands, and prays with us. This Muslim family was among those driven out of Mosul by the Islamic State, and is now living in exile. Their presence serves as a vivid reminder to me that the majority of Iraqi victims of terrorism and displacement are Muslims.

Yousif tells me that Amanuel and Shaba used to play with Omar's children in Mosul – a friendship that neither IS nor religious ideology have been able to destroy. This is encouraging news, given that so many Muslim neighbors betrayed and abandoned their Christian friends when the IS religious fighters invaded Mosul. I am grateful for this example of enduring friendship between Christians and Muslims who refused to let themselves be poisoned by radical Islamic indoctrination. Our conversation over, I take leave of the family, and on impulse offer an unaccustomed deep bow and the words *"salam,* peace," adding *"shukran,* thank you!"

Filled with impressions of the day, I lie down on my couch in the hallway. So many things are still spinning around in my head. Above all, I can't forget Jonah's remark about the neighbors who withdrew their friendship after embracing ultraconservative forms of Islam.

Does religion sometimes destroy our humanity? How is it that Muslims of all people, who pride themselves on their piety, can become capable of inhuman crimes? The perpetrators cite the Koran, where the most recent sura commands: "Do not take the Jews and the Christians for your allies" (5:51). Other verses in the Koran express some degree of goodwill toward Christians and, fortunately, these are taken seriously by many Muslims. Since the "newer" revelations are widely held to supersede the "older" ones, however, the call for hostility toward Christians takes precedence – and this is how hate preachers justify spreading anti-Christian feeling in mosques and inciting their followers to looting and murder. Indeed, numerous fatwas (Islamic legal rulings) have been issued by Salafist or Wahhabi scholars, forbidding any kind of polite or respectful conduct toward Christians on the basis that human friendship with a Christian compromises the purity of the Muslim heart.

View of the Nineveh Plains from Rabban Hormizd Monastery in Alqosh

Above, view from Mar Mattai Monastery looking down the access road
Below, the monastery's dome and cross with Islamic State territory beyond

Church of Mar Gorgees, Ankawa, Iraq

Destruction of Mar Gorgees Church, Mosul, Iraq

Church of Saints Behnam and Sarah, Qaraqosh, Iraq

Inside the Church of Saints Behnam and Sarah

Funeral procession for Archbishop Paulas Faraj Rahho, killed in Mosul in 2008

Below, Syrian Orthodox priests perform the liturgy

A women's choir – an integral part of Syriac liturgy (Church of Mar Yousif, Ankawa)

But how can a religious law have a stronger claim on us than our common humanity? Does this have something to do with the belief in an *absolute* God?

Central to the religions of Judaism, Christianity, and Islam is the belief in one God who is utterly sublime, unknowable, and absolute. This essentially transcendent God reaches out and manifests himself to humanity. According to Judaism, he reveals himself in the creation and in history, notably in the *liberation of the Israelites* from slavery in Egypt. In Christianity, God goes one step further: his revelation culminates in the person of *Jesus of Nazareth*, in whose life, death, and resurrection God is and remains uniquely present. In Islam, finally, God sends his Word down to earth in the form of the *Koran.*

To Muslims, the Arabic text of the Koran is the actual Word of God and, as such, commands absolute respect. From this, conservative Islamic movements derive the claim that the injunctions of the Koran should be taken literally. "Islam" does not, as often maintained, mean "peace," but "devotion" or "submission." Devotion to God is expressed through submission to the divine injunctions.

Christianity, by contrast, is not a book-based religion, even if the Koran describes it as such. God's *Word* was not revealed to the world in a book, but in the person of Jesus of Nazareth. Because the absolute God is present in a *human being,* and because all human beings are an image of that divinity, every person must be respected unconditionally. Part of the uniqueness of Jesus' teachings and conduct is that he puts people before the letter of the law, religious or otherwise, arguing that "the Sabbath was made for man, not man for the Sabbath." Jesus criticizes the perversion of enslaving man in the name of God. Devotion to God is expressed in the act of loving oneself and one's neighbor.

There is no question that the history of Christianity and Islam yields plenty of examples where these patterns are reversed. Sword and Bible-wielding Christians became cruel colonial masters, as reverence for humankind as the image of God gave way to thirst for power in the guise of religion. Conversely, Islam has known periods of relative tolerance. And yet it gives me pause for thought to hear from so many Christians how decades of neighborliness and friendship were destroyed the moment they were declared an enemy on religious grounds.

I shift on my couch. But the tumult isn't just inside my head: it's all around me. Somewhere in the vicinity a TV is humming away softly. Through the door, which doesn't quite fit the doorframe and is merely leaned against it, comes the buzz of conversation from the next room. High and low-pitched voices interweave in an exotic tapestry of sound. Yousif and his family have much to talk about after such a long separation, let alone their bereavement. Luckily, I find a sleep aid among my luggage – some good old-fashioned earplugs. I pop them in and turn over until, overtired, I finally drop off to sleep.

5

A Waiting Game

Next morning straight after breakfast, I telephone the Little
Sisters of Jesus in Ankawa – a community inspired, like
my own, by Charles de Foucauld. One of the older sisters
is from France; the others were born in Iraq, three of them
having lived until recently in Mosul. Now they are living in
a camp among fellow displaced people. They invite me to
visit, and Basman agrees to drive me there.

It has rained in the night and dark clouds herald the
arrival of the next storm with loud claps of thunder. Some
sections of the road are under water, and the car splashes
through the dirty puddles. Amid the wasteland on either
side of us are concrete skeletons and cube-shaped houses,
condemned before they were completed.

We reach the reception camp – one of twenty-two in
Ankawa – and Basman drops me off. At the entrance to
the camp, which is enclosed by a high barbed wire fence,
a couple of men are hanging around. I greet them a little
uneasily with my few words of Arabic, and they give me a
friendly smile. But I don't feel confident until I see Sister
Hannah approaching in the characteristic denim-blue habit
of her order. She is getting on in years, with a wrinkled face
and wavy, graying hair peeping out from her blue headscarf. We greet each other like old friends, and it strikes me
once again how deeply a common spirituality can connect

people. We trudge along the muddy path to the camp,
passing between rows of white containers lined up like
shoe boxes. The rain clouds above us make the gray reality
even grimmer.

There are few people about on the puddle-strewn paths.
In front of some of the containers – constructed from prefab
parts and about the size of a camper – plastic sheeting shelters women selling a variety of household items: brooms,
buckets, cleaning materials, floor cloths. Hannah explains
how people are trying to rebuild their lives. Some have
opened miniature stores, others workshops. I see two young
men making primitive furniture from a stack of pallet
wood. With little work available in Ankawa, these small
activities serve to restore some degree of normality to the
refugees' lives.

About six months ago, 5,600 Christians from Mosul
and Qaraqosh arrived at this camp, having been driven out
of their ancestral homes in the summer of 2014. Looking
around, I see old folk tramping through the mire where
children are playing. Women attempt to sweep the water
out of their containers with brooms, while men are busy
stretching plastic sheeting over the flimsy metal roofs,
which are incapable of withstanding heavy rain. During
the rainy season, the containers turn into dripping caves;
in the summer, they are like furnaces. In July, the tempera-
ture rose to above 127 degrees Fahrenheit, and even the air
conditioners in the containers threatened to overheat.

A child steers an old woman through the mud in a wheelchair. My Iraqi and Syrian friends have told me much about
the camps for refugees and internally displaced people, but
witnessing the scene is infinitely more painful. Hannah
takes me to the container she shares with Sisters Nasrin
and Salama. Scotch-taped to the door is a small cross above
a heart, the logo of our communities. I enter and am again

embraced. The place is simply furnished, with sofa beds along the walls and a corner for prayer and quiet reflection. I feel instantly at home.

This community of Little Sisters lived for many years in Mosul, in the midst of a Christian district with a precious fifth-century church. This age-old center of Christianity had already been in steady decline for years as Islamist extremists ratcheted up the pressure, and incidents of extortion, abduction, rape, and murder began to multiply.

"More and more massacred Christians were being brought into our church for the funeral rites," Hannah tells me. "There was a gradual exodus of Christians from the city, and Iraq in general. By the beginning of 2014, only thirty-five thousand remained in Mosul, out of an original two hundred thousand. In our district, which has a long Christian tradition, there were only five Christian families left, apart from us three sisters. In June we heard that IS militias were approaching the city from the west. But we still had no intention of leaving Mosul."

Fate, however, decided otherwise. On June 10, Muslim neighbors knocked and warned the sisters they had better get out of the city: the IS militias had taken Mosul and the city hall was in flames. That evening, the priest called and asked the sisters to accompany the fleeing Christians. So they each packed a small suitcase and left their community with its beautiful chapel behind. At five o'clock in the morning, they set off on foot to the Tigris bridge which leads to Kurdistan. The further they got, the more the column of refugees swelled. Thousands upon thousands left the city, Christians and Muslims alike.

Salama runs her hands over her small, delicate face.

"I noticed some of the young men were barefoot, which is really unusual here. They must have been soldiers who had thrown away their uniforms, boots and all, to avoid being

shot by the IS militias. One middle-aged man was carrying
an old woman on his back – his mother, perhaps."

Truck beds were overflowing with cases and sacks. On
top of them, old people huddled among sleeping babies
and screaming children. Eventually, the stream of refugees
reached a checkpoint. The sisters thought at first that it
was still patrolled by the Iraqi army, but then they saw the
bearded IS men already in place. That night, no one was
stopped. Day broke on an indescribable scene: a trail of
vehicles and pedestrians crawling eastward along the road,
stretching out across the yellow-brown plain as far as the
eye could see. After walking for three hours, the sisters
reached the border of Iraqi Kurdistan.

"For us, it was exodus and apocalypse all in one," Salama
sighs. "Not only were we leaving our home – we were witnessing the end of the Iraqi Christian world as we knew it."

The facts are indeed depressing: just two years ago,
Mosul's Christian population celebrated Christmas in more
than thirty churches and monasteries. Today, it's possible
that not a single Christian remains in a city where the faith
had flourished for over sixteen hundred years, and which
the leaders of the Islamic State now proudly proclaim a
"Christian-free" zone.

I ask whether any Christians converted to Islam in order
to save their homes and jobs. Hannah says no: there were
plenty of Christians in Mosul who never came to church
but who still wouldn't dream of becoming Muslims. Only a
few bedridden sick and disabled people who had no choice
but to stay renounced their Christian faith and switched to
Islam to avoid being killed.

Hannah goes on to tell me about a very wealthy, childless
couple who managed to reach the checkpoint with large
sums of money and jewelry. A female IS fighter checked the
woman's papers and took all her gold and money away. The

woman asked if she could at least keep a little change to pay
for the bus to the next town and was told, "You can keep all
your money and jewelry and have your nice house back as
well if you become a Muslim." But the woman, who never
came to church, declined.

"What made her do that?" I ask.

Hannah presumes that the value Christianity places on
human life was important to her. Her Christian faith had
taught her that she too – regardless of her sex – had infinite
value. Even if that fact had long slipped into her subconscious, when it came down to it she was in no doubt that she
wanted to remain a Christian, even at the risk of losing her
home and possessions.

My curiosity is still not satisfied. "Tell me more. What
exactly do you mean?"

"Well, our environment is shaped by Islam. The
notion that women are inferior to men is reinforced by
the marriage rule, for example, which says that a man
can marry up to four women. It's the same in everyday
life: women's rights are very limited and subject to male
control. Our Christian culture sees women very differently.
Centuries ago women founded convents here, where they
organized themselves and lived by their own rules. As a
nun, I have plenty of freedom and my value is not defined
in relation to a man or in terms of motherhood. Even as an
unmarried, childless woman, I am accorded the same worth
as any other woman or man. Perhaps this woman I was
telling you about appreciated the Christian view of women
because she was childless herself.

"But back to our journey from Mosul. It was the hottest
part of summer. The air was shimmering with heat, and
some of the older refugees collapsed from exhaustion. After
arriving in Ankawa, people slept in the open at first, then
crammed into small rooms or tents."

On her smartphone, Salama shows me photos of the
courtyard of a church community center in Ankawa.
Sheets of colored fabric are rigged up as partitions. Large
numbers of children sit on the floor among cardboard boxes
and plastic bags. In one picture, a family sits on wooden
benches, glasses of tea in their hands and a vacant look in
their eyes. Men and women stare into space; driven out of
their beloved home, condemned to idleness, and deprived of
a future, they present a picture of sorrow and lethargy.

About a year after their forced migration, Salama tells
me, the Christians were able to move into container settlements erected by the UN Refugee Agency and various
church organizations. At least they now have a reasonably
leak-proof roof over their heads. But their sense of loss runs
deep: "The Mosul Christians were a thriving community:
among them were businesspeople, doctors, teachers, and
all sorts of craftspeople. They have lost everything, and it
has left them anguished and demoralized, with their backs
against the wall. Outwardly, it's true that they are decently
fed and clothed. But deep down inside it's another matter;
there are simply no prospects for the Christian community
in this country. That's the worst of it: having no future in
your own homeland."

Salama's main task is to look after the young people in
the camp. The thirty-six-year-old sister organizes games,
discussions, and courses on Christianity. While Nasrin
is making lunch, Salama takes me on a tour of the camp.
There are schools and improvised soccer pitches for the
children. But today there is no school and no soccer as the
school container is full of water and the sports field actually
under water. The school caretaker shows us the classrooms:
four cramped spaces with narrow benches destined to
remain empty today.

"This school is where migrant teachers teach migrant children – about a hundred girls and boys in total."

I try to do the sums. But then Hannah explains how the school system works. Each child has lessons three days a week. In each room, one class is taught Monday through Wednesday from 7 to 10 a.m., the next from 10 a.m. to 1 p.m., and so on until 7 p.m. The rest of the classes are taught Thursday through Saturday. That way, thirty-two classes can be accommodated in just four rooms.

A few children have gathered in front of the school, and a girl calls out to me. She is slightly disabled and wants to play ball. We throw a red ball back and forth and the girl shouts with glee. Her laughter cuts through the somber atmosphere of this murky day like a voice from another world. I am loath to end the game and leave her.

The children in the camp often ask their parents when they are going home, Hannah tells me. This must be a heartbreaking question to have to answer. Naturally, the children miss their familiar surroundings: their own room with their toys in it, their playmates, their cat, their pet rabbit . . .

In terms of the wider situation, I wonder whether there can ever be any going back. Even if IS is eventually repelled, the Islamization of society as a whole means that Christians will not feel welcome. What good is it to them if the Sunni IS is replaced by a Shiite regime? For years, the country's US-supported Shiite government stood idly by while Christians were bullied, held for ransom, or murdered. Even police officers joined in the attacks. And it was the Shiite Grand Ayatollah of Iraq who issued a fatwa in 2012 compelling the country's Christians to convert to Islam or be outlawed, making it legitimate to kill them. Under the fatwa, which was broadcast on TV, the wife of a Christian also became the rightful property of Muslims, and his daughters too, whether or not they were already married.

All the information I am gathering confirms the lack of equal rights for Christians in Iraq, where Islam is the state religion. This discrimination applies to many areas of life. Even if there is only one Muslim schoolchild in a Christian village, he or she has a right to Muslim religious education. Yet in order for Christianity to be taught in schools, more than 50 percent of the children in a class have to be Christian.

Whether the discrimination is perpetrated by a Sunni or Shiite government makes no difference to the victims. This is the dilemma facing displaced Mosul Christians, hoping on one hand for the city's liberation from the plague of IS, yet fearing the pestilence of another Islamist faction.

Two days before my visit, a church – also in container form – was consecrated in this settlement. Previously, services had been held in a large tent. The priest, who had been exiled with his entire parish, also lives in a container in the camp. In front of the church I come across a group of youths. They crowd around me, wanting to know where I am from. Hannah translates, and they all want to shake my hand. It's only then that I notice a bright eleven-year-old with one sweater sleeve hanging down limply. I get Hannah to ask him how he lost his right arm. "A car bomb in Qaraqosh," he answers. I feel a knot in my stomach at the sight of this poor boy.

Qaraqosh had been the destination of increasing numbers of Christians seeking refuge from the terrorized regions of Iraq. Although less than twenty miles from

Mosul, it had felt a world away from the attacks. But then the Islamic fundamentalists turned their deadly sights on this peaceful, unarmed town as well.

....

Qaraqosh was, until summer 2014, the last of many formerly Christian towns on the Nineveh Plain. It had twelve churches, the oldest dating back to the sixth century, and this long tradition was still very much alive, with twenty-five priests and one hundred and twenty nuns contributing to the local Christian culture. The town even boasted a fourth-century monastery whose origins could be traced back to Saint Behnam (Mar Behnam). The fifty thousand–strong population made a living from agriculture, crafts, and trade. In August 2014, Qaraqosh was overrun by IS militias.

....

It is early in the morning of Tuesday, May 2, 2010. Every day, around twelve hundred students are bused from Qaraqosh to Mosul University, and today is no different. The convoy of eighteen buses is flanked by Iraqi army vehicles. But lurking just in front of a checkpoint on the outskirts of Qaraqosh is a road bomb. A thunderbolt from the ground sends one of the buses flying, as if plucked by an invisible hand. Seconds later, a car bomb explodes beside the next bus. Another ear-splitting bang, and thousands of glass splinters rain down on the young men and women packed into the overcrowded vehicle. A chorus of cries goes up from more than a hundred throats; young, fresh faces are covered with blood. Inside both buses is a blood-smeared chaos of seat upholstery, foam rubber, shredded backpacks, and human body parts. The toll: 180 wounded – many of them scarred for life – and four dead. This attack sent out a signal that people were no longer safe from Islamist terror in Qaraqosh either. The next car bomb incident would claim nine lives.

As we continue our tour, Sister Hannah murmurs, "Wretched car bombs! How many innocent people have been killed by malicious bomb attacks in Iraq over the last few years! Or by suicide bombers trying to take as many victims with them as possible. Often they time the bomb to go off just as Christians are pouring out of church into the street – especially during our major festivals. Such an underhanded strategy."

Hannah knows a lot of people; at every corner we stop and she chats to men, women, and children. Many of the refugees are sick and don't have the money to pay for vital treatments or operations. We visit a few families in their containers, many of which are adorned with a simple wooden cross. There is clearly more to this than slavish tradition; like many generations before them, they have learned the potential consequences of following the crucified Christ. I hear story after story of well-off families suddenly forced to abandon house and home for one reason alone: their Christianity.

What else do they have to cling to but the dream of emigration to Europe, America, or Australia? A dream, but at the same time a nightmare, forcing them to turn their backs – perhaps forever – on their native land. These people face an unbearable dilemma, torn between the desire to stay and the need to leave.

A neighbor knocks to bring the sisters some news, as they don't have a TV. It has just been announced that the UN Refugee Agency is preparing for a new influx of people into Kurdistan, as the Iraqi army prepares for a joint advance on Mosul with the peshmerga forces in a bid to free the city from IS. Will I see any of this during the last four days of my stay? Or is the whole thing mere propaganda?

This much I know: the people here are stuck in limbo between the darkness of despair and the occasional faint ray of hope.

6

When They Persecute You

Next morning, Sister Salama again makes time for me. She
is from a village in northern Iraq that used to be inhabited
by Christians and Kurds. When the Iraqi army bombarded
Kurdistan in 1968, it was not only the Kurds who lost
their homes in large numbers, but also Christians who
had nothing to do with the conflict. Of the 180 Christian
villages in the north of Iraq, some 150 were razed to the
ground. In recent years, Turkey has likewise attacked Iraqi
Kurds, shelling a few unarmed Christian villages in the
process and prompting many Christians to flee abroad.
Salama is the only member of her family still living in Iraq;
all the others are scattered across four continents.

From the camp, we cross half-finished roads lined with
never-to-be-finished houses and, after walking for some
distance, we reach the center of old Ankawa. First, Salama
shows me the Church of Mar Gorgees (Saint George). The
oriental dome topped with a cross reveals at a glance that
this is an ancient church: the dome symbolizes the celes-
tial vault, suggesting to believers that the celebration of
the liturgy will bring them closer to heaven. The interior
of the mighty-pillared building, which dates back to 816,
is illuminated by a chalky light and plainly decorated: no
pictures, just a cross above the altar. Salama explains that
Christianity came to Ankawa as early as the first century.

The nearby city of Erbil was then known as Arbela, and had been an important diocesan town since AD 104. The gospel has been preached and practiced here for over nineteen hundred years.

Over the last decade, the Christian village of Ankawa has evolved into a smallish town with a population of around thirty thousand. Many Christians from Baghdad or Mosul sought refuge in the Kurdish autonomous region, some still cherishing the hope that Iraq might revert to normality at some point, and that they would be able to return to their homes and jobs. This prompted the construction of numerous row house developments, along with high-rise buildings, shopping malls, and churches, interspersed with hotels, sports centers, and entertainment complexes for the foreign oil workers.

I ask Salama how many Christians there are in Ankawa now. She tells me that thousands upon thousands of Christians from places like Baghdad have been fleeing to Kurdistan for many years, though no one knows how many are still living here. On top of that, tens of thousands of Christians sought sanctuary in this small town in June 2014, after being driven out of Mosul and the surrounding area. Some of them had initially fled to Qaraqosh, but when the IS militia seized control there too, they were forced to decamp further eastward, together with those who had harbored them. Another hundred thousand or so refugees arrived in Kurdistan overnight. Most of the total of 350,000 Christians from Mosul and the neighboring Nineveh Plain are probably still in Kurdistan: in Ankawa, Duhok, Zakho, and villages further to the north. But anyone who can flees further afield.

Next, Salama wants to show me the Ankawa Mall. The road leading there is very busy, so we trudge along the wet, muddy strip that passes for a grass verge. A few minutes

later, we find ourselves in front of a huge building complex.
The planned shopping mall was never completed, and the
entrance to the half-finished yet outwardly smart building
is boarded up.

"Countless refugees were given temporary accommodation in this building. Imagine living in a place that gets no
daylight and looks like an underground garage. They put
up partitions between the rough concrete walls to give the
families at least some sense of security and protection. It
was amazing to see people celebrate Christmas with their
children in this concrete block."

Salama gets out her phone and searches for some photos.
I look at the images: Christmas in a windowless shell;
hundreds of children in a hall "festively" trimmed with
a few balloons; long rows of small plush toys on a table
awaiting distribution. I am touched by the children's faces
as they sit expectantly on their cheap plastic chairs, waiting
for their Christmas presents. Another photo shows a red
Santa Claus in front of a gray concrete wall.

"Where are they now, the people who were in the mall?" I
ask uneasily.

"Some of them are living in hurriedly thrown-up
tenement blocks. Others are still spread around the refugee
camps."

We visit one of these camps not far from the Ankawa
Mall, in the grounds of Mar Elya Church. Right by the
entrance we come across a small playground where a gaggle
of shrieking children are charging around concrete table
tennis tables. Salama and I sit down on a rather fragile
bench and watch in amusement as the kids let off steam.

"It's the children who keep us going," I hear Salama
murmur.

I give her a sideways look. She notices and continues, "You know, without the children we'd all have despaired long ago and fallen into a deep depression. The people have lost everything and it's unlikely they'll be able to return home. Even in Kurdistan they can't stay forever. But where can they go? They can't afford to pay people-smugglers. And only a few countries are taking in refugees. In a hopeless situation like this, the children are the only ray of light – playing, laughing, breathing life. Their joy is still untroubled by thoughts about the future. They don't worry about tomorrow: they live in the here and now. Look how engrossed they are in their game!"

Her words make me all the more appreciative of the children's antics – their ringing laughter and enthusiastic cries. And when they invite me and Salama to join in the game, we race around the table with the others, and for a moment I am able to forget the cheerless surroundings of the camp.

Abuna Rayan, the priest of the small Mar Elya Church, had this settlement built to house around a hundred families. The containers are closer together than in the other camp, and I weave my way through the narrow alleys with Salama. All around us children are playing, laundry is drying on fences, and women and men alike are cooking on gas stoves. A smell of frying onions, garlic, and spices floats on the air. In one container, some women sit in a circle making dumplings with deft hands. There are no toilets or running water in the containers: for that you have to go to the camp perimeter. By contrast, we are shown one container fitted out with sewing machines, one with computers, and one serving as a hair salon – an attempt to provide at least some measure of occupation for the camp residents while they wait for their fate to be decided. So far it's been a year and a half – and counting.

Abuna Rayan is currently trying to obtain visas for the Christians from Qaraqosh. Slovakia has agreed to take ten families, Mexico twenty. For those thirty families, that means the hope of a future. But it comes at a cost: the fragmentation of families, friends, culture, and church.

It's a bleak picture: the "last Christians" are sitting on packed suitcases, if they have one to their name. If I've interpreted what I've heard correctly, even Kurdistan can't offer them a permanent home. There are few jobs available, and to get one you need to speak Kurdish, whereas the Christians speak Aramaic or Arabic.

Compounding this problem is a deep-seated mistrust. For centuries, Kurds bullied and attacked Christians and violated Christian women and girls. Nowadays, they operate on a policy of tolerance. On the global political stage, the way a nation treats minorities matters if it wants to be recognized as a state. But once the Kurds have established their own state, will they continue to respect Christians as equal citizens? Certainly, there are secular political parties in Kurdistan, and Christians currently enjoy a degree of freedom and security found in few other Muslim-ruled places. But even here they face certain disadvantages as non-Kurds and non-Muslims. Worst of all, they are exposed to the poison of religious fanaticism. Imams of the Kurdistan Islamic Union, which has close links with the Muslim Brotherhood, incite their followers against Christians, banning Muslims from working on "Christian" building sites, for example – even in the case of humanitarian projects.

I remember reading that, not long ago, an inflamed Muslim mob looted and destroyed Christian shops and businesses – notably hairdressers – after being told at a

Friday sermon that it is an offence to Islam for a Christian to shave the beard of a Muslim.

After the riots, the government of Iraqi Kurdistan ordered the arrest of some of the looters and saw to it that the Christians concerned were compensated. Nevertheless, many Christians doubt that they will be able to live here safely in the long term, and therefore tend to regard Kurdistan merely as a stepping stone to Europe or America. I am reminded of a line from the Gospel of Matthew which is painfully apt in the circumstances: "When they persecute you in one town, flee to the next" (10:23).

At the end of our tour, I ask Salama to accompany me to the Church of Mar Yousif.

"Gladly," she nods. "But how did you know about it? And why do you want to see it?"

"The architect who designed it lives in Leipzig. He doesn't know I'm in Ankawa. I'd like to surprise him with a photo of his church."

Salama looks at me curiously, and I start to tell her the story.

7

A Life's Work in Ruins

Among the guests at the Charles de Foucauld memorial service that my fellow brothers and I hosted at our parish community center nearly a year ago was an older gentleman with his wife. During the evening, I sat down at their table and they invited me with an irresistible smile to visit them in Paunsdorf. The hospitality of Eastern refugees never fails to impress me: I have lived in Leipzig for ten years now and have many good friends there, but rarely am I invited to anyone's home.

Paunsdorf, like Grünau, is one of Leipzig's prefab housing projects, but smaller and at the other end of the city. It's a few weeks before I finally get round to following up the couple's generous invitation and find myself rattling across the city to the streetcar terminus. Disembarking, I wander around between concrete blocks looking for the street and house number I've been given. Eventually, the exotic name "Ziyad Hani" on a doorbell panel tells me I have come to the right place.

Ziyad invites me into their small apartment and asks me to sit down on the blue sofa in the living room. On the dresser opposite are some silver-framed wedding and baby photos, along with a snapshot of Ziyad's eldest son, Adnan, who happens to be sitting across from me. Adnan lives in Berlin and has come to visit his parents today. He

works for a logistics company and speaks excellent German,
unlike his father, who has difficulty mastering our unwieldy
tongue. But the seventy-five-year-old Ziyad is undeterred,
and I learn during our conversation that he is working
steadily on improving his language skills. For the last couple
of months, he has had a retired teacher from a Catholic
parish over to help him practice reading and speaking with
the aid of a children's Bible, whose simple language and
familiar content make it an ideal learning resource. Ziyad's
wife Raneen also finds German a struggle, but she compen-
sates by expressing her friendliness through her face and
gestures – a language that needs no words.

While I chat with Ziyad and Adnan, Raneen withdraws
and busies herself in the kitchen. Soon, the aroma of Arabic
coffee permeates the apartment, and my eyes begin to
wander to the homemade candy arranged invitingly in a
bowl on the coffee table.

Ziyad is a quiet, elderly man with a quintessential Arab
face. He and his wife have lived in Paunsdorf for over four
years, but this world is still alien to him, he tells me with a
sad shake of the head. Back home in Mosul, people's doors
were always open – neighbors, friends, and acquaintances
were constantly dropping in or inviting you back to their
homes. Here, by contrast, none of the neighbors have ever
spoken to him or asked him over after all this time. Even
in the local Catholic church, which he and his wife attend
regularly, they are acknowledged with a friendly nod, but
nothing more. Thankfully, he has recently struck up a
relationship with the teacher who is helping him with his
German. But besides this teacher, I am only the second
German to visit Ziyad's home.

There is an echo of disappointment in the old man's
words. After his German evening classes, it would have
been useful to have contact with native speakers in order to

practice this unfamiliar new language in everyday life. But
no one engages with him or his wife. This sets me thinking
about my own environment, and how seldom I've been
proactive toward people who are obviously foreign and
perhaps still getting a grip on our language and culture.
And it occurs to me how often we Germans rave about
the spontaneous hospitality we enjoy when holidaying in
southern countries: how ready people are to talk to us, help
us, or invite us to their homes. Why, then, do we find it so
difficult to learn from our experiences abroad and apply the
lesson at home?

Meanwhile, Raneen has joined us around the table and we
sip the hot, sweet, thick coffee. I ask about the photos and
learn that Ziyad's family is scattered across the globe: a
daughter in the States, a son in Sweden, Adnan in Berlin.
Other relatives are in Kurdistan waiting for a chance to
settle in some corner of the world. Once again, I am in the
presence of a family torn apart by war and terror.

Ziyad has an extremely polite manner, and gives the
impression of having lived a peaceful, contented life. But I
soon learn that this is not the case; his story is one of fear,
flight, and destruction, though he tells it with amazing
restraint.

Ziyad is from Mosul, where he worked as an architect.
He designed eight churches, an indication of the relative
freedom enjoyed by Iraqi Christians under the secular
dictator Saddam Hussein, Iraq being one of the few Islamic
countries where the construction of churches was allowed.

But what became of Ziyad's life's work? Adnan places
a laptop on the living room table and enters some Arabic
words in the Google search box. An imposing building
appears on the screen: Mosul's Cathedral Church of
Saint Ephrem. It boasts an exotic style blending modern

architectural elements with classical oriental forms. I
remark on the fascinating structure of its dome. In a choked
voice, Ziyad tells me that the Islamic religious fighters
have since turned the building into what is now known as
the "Mosque of the Mujahideen." The next image shows
what happened to the cross that once towered above the
entrance: its side arms severed, the body now serves as a
huge mast to which a black flag with the IS crest has been
tied. The white lettering on it, Adnan explains to me, is the
Islamic creed, the same creed that adorns the Saudi Arabian
national flag. The similarity between the two banners could
hardly be coincidental.

Ziyad also built a church in Qaraqosh, named after
Saints Behnam and Sarah and consecrated in 2008. Once
again, I am impressed by the combination of oriental
and modern architecture. Ziyad shows me a picture of
the packed interior when 238 children took their First
Communion.

Today, however, both Mosul and Qaraqosh are, in the
cynical terminology of IS, "Christian-free." What this
church is used for now, Ziyad cannot bring himself to say.
His already quiet voice becomes even more subdued and he
is unable to hide his grief. Raneen, who is silently perusing
the photos with us, has tears running down her cheeks.

The last of Ziyad's churches was commissioned by
Mosul's Armenian community. After three years the
building, inspired by classical forms of Armenian architecture, was almost completed. But in 2013, a month before it
was due to be consecrated, the church was destroyed by an
Islamist bomb. Now Ziyad too is struggling to hold back the
tears. And yet not a bitter or accusing word escapes his lips,
despite the intense pain written on his face.

Since June 2014, IS militias have ransacked more than
thirty churches, turning them into mosques, setting them

on fire, or blowing them up, as in the case of the Church of the Virgin Mary, one of the largest and oldest churches in Mosul. Where the cross on domes and spires once proclaimed Jesus' message of peace even in his death, the black banner of IS now flies, threatening terror and violence.

Only one of the eight churches designed by Ziyad is still used for Christian worship: Mar Yousif in Ankawa. Ziyad explains that he chose the Babylonian style for this church: instead of having a dome at the center, it takes the form of a ziggurat, with battlements tapering toward the top. The entrance – an arch framed by two towers – recalls the city gates of ancient Babylon.

I like Ziyad's openness to the styles of other cultures and his desire to value and preserve them. What a contrast to the puritanical Islam preached by the Muslim Brotherhood, Wahhabis, and Salafists, under whom archaeologically important ruins are demolished, ancient Christian books burned, and even mosques blown up because of the Christian elements they contain! Adnan tells me his family used to live less than two miles away from the Mosque of the Prophet Jonah. This had originally been the site of a Christian cathedral, which was later turned into a mosque frequented by Jews, Christians, and Muslims alike – until, in 2014, IS razed this interfaith beacon to the ground.

The things I am hearing set me pondering: Does the destructiveness of radical Muslims in Syria, Iraq, Turkey, and Saudi Arabia reveal a subconscious fear of acknowledging that Islam didn't just appear from nowhere? It cannot, after all, be denied that Islam's origins lie in other traditions. The Koran borrows much from the Bible and the Syriac Christian liturgy; the typical domed mosque is copied from Eastern churches such as the Hagia Sophia;

and the minarets associated with mosques echo the church spires of early Christian buildings. The orientation of the mosque in a particular direction, the act of praying several times a day, and the praying posture itself are direct legacies of Judaism and Christianity which have been modified to give them a Muslim-specific character. Just as the Jews observe the Sabbath, and Christians Sunday, as their rest day, Muhammad chose Friday as the Muslim holy day. Even the mystic prayer rituals of the Sufis can be traced back to Christian monks.

Perhaps this close relationship helps to explain the dispute over the family inheritance – and the fact that such a murderous hatred of Jews and Christians was able to develop within certain currents of Islam. Does this hatred act like a kind of autoimmune disease, leading Muslims to reject part of their own heritage?

Psychologists might cite the motive of "matricide" in this context: a religion that is "born" of another and inherits many of its characteristics seeks to break free and refuses to be bound by or reminded of its origins. After all, for the new religion to supersede the old one, the latter must eventually die – hence the conversion of churches into mosques and the long history of forced Islamization. In recent times, this "matricide" phenomenon has been brutally apparent in IS's destruction of anything that harks back to Islam's ancestry: age-old churches and monasteries that stand as a testimony to Christianity's influence on Islam are blown up and bulldozed into the ground.

Meanwhile, Raneen has returned to the kitchen, and the sounds and smells emanating from it suggest that something more substantial is in preparation. I wasn't really intending to stay this long, but I can't turn down the

invitation to supper now. Besides, I am glad of the opportunity to hear Adnan relate how he and his family came to
Germany.

Adnan studied English in Mosul and worked as an interpreter while Saddam Hussein's government was still in
power. As an English-Arabic translator, he found himself
increasingly called on by Iraqi intelligence agencies. At
that time, Western secret services were attempting to spy
on Saddam Hussein's regime and there were signs that a
war was in the offing. Adnan became privy to intelligence
operations and military projects, and this made him feel
increasingly ill at ease. He knew too much and wasn't willing
to die for it. So he looked for an opportunity to abscond
abroad. After hurriedly gaining an interpreting qualification
in Turkish, he found a job with UNESCO in Erbil. From
there, he traveled to Turkey on a legal passport and managed
to make his way to Istanbul. He figured that if he were to
get a flight out of Turkey, the Iraqi intelligence agency would
soon be on his tail, so he opted to pay a people-smuggling
gang 7,500 euros to take him across the sea to Italy. In
September 2001, he got on a boat bound for Calabria. The
small vessel only had space for a hundred people, but set out
across the Mediterranean with 220 on board.

After several weeks on the open sea amid the constant
threat of storms, the boat was eventually discovered by the
Italian coast guard and allowed to moor in Otranto. Instead
of registering there as arranged, Adnan slipped off as
soon as he reached land, his plan being to get to Germany.
He walked, bused, and hitched his way to Rome, then on
to Genoa, and from there to Ventimiglia on the French-
Italian border. Together with twelve other refugees – most
of them Kurds – he climbed onto a freight train and clung
on between the cars. That way they managed to cross the
border, but were caught immediately and arrested on the

French side. While Adnan was being searched, one of the border officials noticed he was wearing a small cross and, taking him aside, asked whether he was a Christian. When Adnan confirmed this, and the fact that he was from Iraq, the French border guard gave him a tip: "We have to send you back now. If you want to try again, go on foot through the railway tunnel just before the border. But be careful: it's dangerous!"

He was then duly returned to Italy with the other arrested refugees. The handover took place according to strict military protocol: a delegation of border police from both countries marched toward no man's land, the French side leading thirteen handcuffed men. At the border, the French handcuffs were exchanged for Italian ones, the border guards saluted each other, and the refugees were led away by the Italian police. The French were barely out of sight when the Italians stopped, removed the handcuffs, and advised the refugees that there were better ways of crossing the border, and that they would be better off going to Germany than France. Adnan already had his insider tip, however, and kept it to himself.

The next night, he cautiously approached the small railway tunnel close to the cliff edge. With the waves crashing onto the rocks below him, he scrambled over bushes and boulders until he reached the tunnel entrance. There he found three more new refugees, and the four of them spent some time observing the rhythm of the trains as they rattled through. They calculated that they had just under ten minutes between trains to run along the tracks through the tunnel, which they reckoned to be just over half a mile long. As soon as the next train had cleared the tunnel, they charged after it. The coarse gravel and dim lighting made progress slower than they had hoped. With another train already approaching from behind, the four

marshaled all their strength and just managed to leap off
the tracks in time.

Adnan walked as far as Nice, then made his way to Paris.
What vastly different worlds he encountered along the way!
Before his escape, he had never been out of Iraq. Now here
he was, crossing cities like Rome, Genoa, Nice, and Paris.
The next stop was The Hague, from where he finally made it
via Aachen to Cologne. There he reported to the police and
was locked in a cell for six hours. After that, he applied for
asylum, which he was soon granted.

A deep anxiety still plagued him, however: because he
had absconded after being entrusted with confidential
information, something might happen to his family in
Mosul. Adnan knew that phone calls were monitored in
Iraq, so he could only send news indirectly. Then, out of the
blue, his family was asked to pass on a message to him: he
was to report to a certain person in Bonn. Now he knew
he'd been tracked down and that his life could be on the
line. To avoid any risk to his family in Mosul, he accepted
the invitation to meet a "colleague" from Iraq. With strained
nerves and beating heart, Adnan presented himself at
the appointed office building. His contact turned out to
be sympathetic, advising him to lay low and avoid notice.
Adnan was overcome with relief. Shortly afterwards, the
United States launched an attack on Iraq with the aim of
toppling Saddam Hussein, and he realized the reason for the
message: the staff of the intelligence unit in Bonn had probably already sensed that Saddam's days were numbered, and
were giving Adnan the all-clear. With the fall of Saddam
Hussein's regime and the destruction of his secret service,
Adnan was finally free.

His family in Mosul, however, was faced with a new
danger, as radical Islamic groups began to terrorize Christians. First, a threatening letter arrived, demanding a large

sum in protection money. Ziyad paid up, hoping it would buy him peace and security, but a second demand followed soon after. Ziyad and Raneen hastily packed a few things and drove to Syria. In Damascus, they rented a small apartment and registered with the UN Refugee Agency, which they learned about by chance. At the same time, they hoped that the situation in Mosul would calm down again. From Damascus, Ziyad arranged payment of a second sum to the Islamists. Then he and his wife drove back to Mosul in the hope of being allowed to stay in their home city.

But attacks on Mosul Christians increased, and the propaganda in the mosques seethed with hatred. First an uncle of Ziyad's was abducted, then one of his brothers. Threatening letters landed in his mailbox, accusing him of the sin of building Christian churches. With a heavy heart, the elderly couple decided to escape to Syria a second time. In Damascus they found help forthcoming from the UN: because their son Adnan had gained a foothold in Germany, they were able to obtain a visa via the German embassy and were allocated to the asylum seeker hostel in Chemnitz.

After being treated to an ample supper of Middle Eastern specialties, I bid farewell to the kindhearted couple and to Adnan, who has put down firm roots in Germany and is currently building a house near Berlin. He tells me this in a slightly anxious tone and goes on to confide, "A few days ago I told my wife we'd soon be able to move into our new home. But in ten or fifteen years' time, IS will come and drive us out again." I shake my head as I take my leave, but Adnan's last remark stays with me long afterward.

His words come back to me now as I sit on my couch in Ankawa, clicking through the photos I took of Ziyad's

church today. I'm sure Ziyad will be pleased to see the one
of me standing by the entrance. Outside, a thunderstorm
is breaking, echoing my inner disquiet. The power goes off
again, and the lightning flashes are my only light source for
the next few minutes.

From the multipurpose living/dining/bedroom comes
a clatter of dishes. A little later, the light comes back on
and I join Yousif and his mother for supper. A Muslim
family comes to visit: a young woman in a headscarf, a tall
man, and three small children. They sit on the sofas and
Yousif introduces Hamoudi to me: "We were neighbors in
Mosul – and very good friends."

Then I hear Hamoudi's story. He tells me how IS terrorists captured Yazidi women and children and deported
them to Mosul for their "own use," imprisoning them in
different houses. Hamoudi managed to rescue a fourteen-
year-old girl and fled with her and his own family to
Kurdistan. In my opinion, this man deserves some kind
of honor, just as people who rescued Jews in the Third
Reich were honored as the "Righteous among the Nations."
Because of his brave action, he is now living in exile and
cannot return to Mosul.

This story brings home to me yet again how many Muslims
have been at the receiving end of Islamist terrorism. And I
am very glad to have met a Muslim who put his own life on
the line to help an "unbeliever." Muslims like Hamoudi, who
crave democracy and respect for human rights, have been
forced to flee their homelands and seek asylum in Germany.
In Leipzig, I met a young Muslim mechanic who fled to
Germany in peril of his life rather than agree to work on a
project designing car bombs.

It saddens and angers me to think of such Muslims
becoming victims of blind Islamophobia. At the same time,

I am aware that I am not always discerning enough myself. To do greater justice to this complex reality, we need to look at it far more closely. There are so many Muslims who come to Europe precisely because they don't want a Salafist Islam. They have suffered greatly under the dictatorial systems of their native countries, which often pervert the ideology of Islam, and they want to be free at last to experience a different political and social culture. They need my – and our – support, in order to give succor to those currents within Islam that reject discrimination against non-Muslims and violence in the name of religion.

If we can succeed in integrating these people, we will have taken an important step toward humanizing our world and increased the chances of non-fundamentalist forms of Islam spreading. People like Hamoudi deserve our wholehearted support, because they champion respect and human dignity based on a tolerant reading of the Koran.

Hamoudi gives me an insight into everyday life in Mosul under the tyranny of IS: a man who shaves receives ten blows with the rod; anyone caught with a cell phone, ten blows. At school, children now learn their tables using the symbols of war: one grenade plus another grenade equals two grenades. Even the plus sign is replaced by another symbol because of its resemblance to a cross. And sports education has been renamed "jihad training."

The "jihadization" of school lessons subjects children to brainwashing from a young age in order to instill Salafist ideology and hatred of Christians. A regime that kills children is also training them to kill other children.

Hamoudi tells me about other measures. At the University of Mosul, departments such as archaeology, political science, and art have been closed down. All subjects relating to democracy, culture, or secular law are prohibited.

Anyone who protests is executed. And at the university library, all works written by Christians are weeded out since, in the eyes of the Salafists, only Muslims can know the truth.

....

Jihad translates literally as "effort" or "striving." In the Koran, "jihad" is used in more than 80 percent of cases to mean "waging a war in the name of religion." The idea that those who die for the cause go straight to paradise as martyrs also appears in the Koran.

The concept of religious war, to which Muhammad attached particular importance in the context of self-defense, later came to be interpreted in an aggressive sense, and even promoted to the status of a supreme religious act.

Once Islamic rule over the Middle East and southern Mediterranean had been established in the eighth century, jihad took on a more spiritual meaning, and the sense of military engagement on behalf of God became less important. Mystics in particular championed a statement attributed to Muhammad distinguishing between "greater jihad" (the effort to lead a perfect religious life) and "lesser jihad" (armed struggle). But even in subsequent centuries, there have always been scholars keen to hark back to the duty to engage in aggressive jihad and spread Islam by military means. The doctrine of a holy war is one of the hallmarks of Islam, and its impact – on jihadists of all persuasions, among them women – continues to be felt to this day. In 2014, on average, 168 people a day were killed by jihadist attacks.

....

8

A Bishop in Exile

The rain is lashing down, drumming on the tin roof under which Yousif's relatives have left their old cars. My friend appears to be a talented mechanic; at least, his family has plenty of confidence in his ability to get their rust buckets back on the road again. Since Yousif has his hands full, Uncle Wadid takes me to see Bishop Petros Mouche, whom I had read about in *Die Zeit* and managed to contact via the Little Sisters.

Petros Mouche is – or rather was – the Bishop of Qaraqosh. Until recently, this city formed the hub of an area where Christians were still in the majority and spoke their native Aramaic tongue. Bishop Petros had originally lived in Mosul, but the proliferation of attacks on Christians prompted him to move his residence to Qaraqosh some years ago, until he was driven away again. Now he no longer has a residence at all, but lives on the outskirts of Ankawa, where the desert begins.

Uncle Wadid calls a friend for directions. With the windshield wipers on full speed, we splash through huge puddles, sending up showers of spray. After zigzagging our way along the flooded roads, we eventually reach the edge of town and drive on between building sites. On the left-hand side is a refugee camp made up of white metal boxes. "That's where

they housed the Yazidis who fled from the Islamic State,"
Uncle Wadid tells me, but that's all he knows.

We wind up on a dead-end street in one of the ubiquitous
half-finished settlements – yet another abandoned building
project steadily sinking into decay, with rusty iron rods
thrusting out of concrete pillars like spines. We stop to ask
the way, but there is no one around in this foul weather.
Falling back on the phone for guidance, we strike out along
a muddy cart track into the desert. This treeless, shrubless
landscape looks even bleaker in the gray drizzle.

....

The **Yazidis** are a small religious community living mainly in the
north of Iraq. They are monotheists (believing in a single god)
and have no holy book, but only oral traditions. Throughout
their history, they have been subject to persecution by Muslim
rulers, being regarded as "unbelievers." Islamic State militias
have likewise expelled, enslaved, or murdered many Yazidis.

....

Finally, we arrive at a construction site in the middle of
nowhere. The plan is to establish a small center for the
Syriac Catholic "diocese of Mosul, Qaraqosh, and Kurdistan." Part of the building is already complete and occupied
by Bishop Petros Mouche, whom I have arranged to meet
today, Wednesday, November 11, 2015. Bidding farewell to
Wadid, I dash through the rain to the entrance.

Bishop Petros Mouche is seventy-two years old. His striking
round face is framed by a full head of short, silver-white hair
and a neat beard; his black eyes contemplate the world sadly
from under bushy brows. I follow him into a large room
where we sit down. It's damp and cool, and I am glad of the
hot tea brought to us by a young, sporty-looking priest who
serves as the bishop's secretary. We speak in French, and

I ask them to describe what happened to them and their church.

"The Islamic State robbed me of my diocese," the bishop laments. "When the terrorists overran Mosul on the night of June 9, 2014, the Iraqi army fled for their lives, leaving the city to fend for itself. After a few weeks I was summoned, along with other church leaders, to appear before the IS commanders. It was clear to us that this was a trap, so we didn't respond. Not long after, shari'a law was proclaimed over the loudspeakers of the mosques. Christians were to convert to Islam or pay protection money. Otherwise, they would be given twenty-four hours to leave. After that, almost all of Mosul's Christians fled their home city in panic."

The move was not without its opponents. Bishop Petros speaks with great respect of the Sunni university professor Mahmoud al-Asali, who protested publicly against the Christians' expulsion and was brutally murdered. But ultimately, the bishop and his fellow Christians were left with no choice but to relocate to Qaraqosh, the last bastion of Aramaic-speaking Christians. Petros Mouche's house in Mosul was burned down and the residence of the Syriac Orthodox bishop appropriated by IS.

Bishop Petros relates what happened next to the Mosul Christians. Shortly after the jihadists seized the city, peshmerga troops advanced into the Nineveh Plain. The president of the autonomous region of Kurdistan declared that the peshmerga would defend the town of Qaraqosh – as the "gateway to Erbil," it was held to be of strategic importance for the security of Kurdistan. At the end of June, heavy fighting broke out between the peshmerga forces and IS, causing most of the 120,000 Christians from the Nineveh Plain to flee to Kurdistan. The peshmerga managed to hold their positions, and the heavy guns eventually fell silent. With the battle seemingly over, Bishop Petros called for the faithful to return to their houses in Qaraqosh, which many duly did.

On August 6, IS troops began another push eastward toward Kurdistan. Water and power supplies to Qaraqosh were cut and fighting erupted again between IS and the peshmerga. The boom of guns and rumors of another onslaught threw the Qaraqosh Christians into a state of anxiety.

The bishop relates the story of a young mother who was in her front yard with her two young children when an ear-piercing whistle rent the air; seconds later, shells began to rain down on Qaraqosh. The explosion tore through the bodies of both children and their mother. The three victims were buried at the cemetery that afternoon, as the news of an impending IS attack filtered through.

The peshmerga assured Bishop Petros that they would defend the town against IS and, as evening approached, he called the local community representatives together to inform them that they could count on the Kurdish fighters' protection. But the opposite proved to be the case: just before midnight, the IS troops advanced out of the blue on an utterly defenseless town, the Kurdish troops having withdrawn beforehand. Qaraqosh became a scene of chaos. The many Christians from Mosul who had managed to flee there with a few remaining belongings left the last of their worldly possessions behind in this second exodus. Many simply started running at random, in the hope of finding safety. The surrounding villages too had been abandoned without protection. In the middle of the night, an endless column of refugees set off in the direction of Erbil. Bishop Petros and the local priests were among the last to leave the town.

Many Christians were robbed en route by IS "holy warriors"; even their marriage certificates and land ownership certificates had to be surrendered. Bishop Petros told me of one eighty-year-old man who asked the terrorists why they wouldn't spare his family any food for the children; their response was to hack off his hands and feet. The few people who stayed behind in Qaraqosh suffered a similar fate. Bishop Petros heard that one man had his eyes gouged out and his nine-year-old son tied to a car and dragged through the streets.

What pains Bishop Petros most of all is his community's loss of trust in their Muslim neighbors. "I say this from bitter experience – especially the way Sunni Arabs from the surrounding villages betrayed us to IS. They even joined forces with the fanatics. We were cruelly disappointed to see our Muslim friends and neighbors looting our towns and villages."

The young priest adds with a sigh: "In Mosul, too, we Christians waited in vain for help from Muslim friends we'd lived side by side with for many years. Not even a text message of solidarity! As Louis Raphael I, the patriarch of Baghdad, rightly asked, where was the outcry from the Islamic world when over a hundred thousand Christians were expelled in a single night in the name of Islam? How many imams protested when ancient churches or monasteries were blown to bits? It's shocking how weak and feeble the official Islamic world has been in its reaction to this violence against Christians."

The young man, who has studied in Rome, quotes a Latin proverb: "He who says nothing implies consent."

After a brief silence, he continues: "How can we rebuild our trust? We can't simply forget what happened. And how can there be a reconciliation with our Muslim neighbors when they haven't expressed the slightest regret? Indeed, will Muslims ever be capable of acknowledging any guilt toward us Christians?"

Bishop Petros intervenes quietly at this point: "In times like these we ourselves can experience feelings of aggression. We must overcome them. It is God's will that we should love our enemies!"

I am silent, left speechless by his stance in the face of such a brutal reality. He shakes his head thoughtfully. "We can't just forget what has happened. But we will ask God to forgive the offenders and lead them to think differently."

Still, the white-haired bishop's face betrays a deep anguish. With this last oasis of Iraqi Christianity now under IS control, and a nearly two-thousand-year-old local church reduced to rubble, Qaraqosh is like a ghost town. Bishop Petros is especially troubled by the fate of a three-year-old girl and some young women abducted from the Christian villages of the Nineveh Plain who – like the Yazidi women – face sexual abuse, forced marriage with Islamic fighters, and slavery.

Because the Kurds feared that IS terrorists might infiltrate the refugee columns to gain access to Kurdistan, the Christians who finally made it to the border had to enter on foot with nothing but the clothes they were wearing. So the newly arrived refugees had no food, no extra clothes, and no medication. Grown men were seen standing in the road and weeping.

The bishop laments the fact that, after fleeing Qaraqosh in such a panic, the twelve thousand families were then dispersed around fifty-seven different camps or communities. Among these was the small Church of Mart Shmony in Ankawa. Utterly exhausted from trekking ten to twenty miles in the blistering summer heat, people slept both inside the church and on the forecourt. Next morning,

Bishop Petros held a service on the spot, confessing in tears how he had been deceived: "They let you down, and they let me down." This accusation was directed at the peshmerga, but also, more particularly, at the Iraqi government in Baghdad for its failure to protect a peaceable Christian people that had never gone to war in its two-thousand-year history. At first, the refugees slept out in the desert-like fields, in churches and schools, or in the shells of unfinished buildings. Food was prepared on the ground, using old newspapers as tablecloths. There were no toilets, and in some cases up to twenty people – men, women, and children – were crammed together in one room for months, an unbearable situation that bred tension and depression.

Listening to the bishop's account, I can hear the weariness between the words. He, too, lived together with seven families – a total of forty-seven people – in one house. They slept in shifts; the bishop was allocated a bed from eleven in the evening till five in the morning, then it was the next person's turn. Later, tent cities were erected, and after about ten months the container settlements were completed. "We opened medical stations with the help of our physicians and the support of church charities. And we set up schools so that our teachers could return to the classroom. The children have to be given the chance of a future."

The secretary takes up the thread: "Our bishop remained among his people and lived, like us priests, in a container. We have now re-established church communities in the camps – three days ago, a container church was consecrated in one of them."

Bishop Petros nods: "My diocese now has a place of worship once again, if only a makeshift one. And as you can see, I am now living in the new center of my diocese – in the middle of a building site!"

He continues: "Over the last sixteen months, we have christened some six hundred children and celebrated four hundred twenty weddings in the various camps where the Syriac Catholic Christians are scattered. But what kind of future do they have? Should I encourage people to stay here in the face of so much insecurity? Should I hope for Qaraqosh or Mosul to be liberated from IS's reign of terror?" Here Bishop Petros shrugs helplessly. "Or should I send our Christians into exile and encourage them to emigrate to Europe, America, or Australia? We don't want to leave. This soil is sacred and precious to us, imbued with the blood of our ancestors, who suffered so much violence because of their Christian beliefs yet never let themselves be infected by it. And the same goes for Christians today – they may have lost everything else, but they have never lost their faith."

With some bitterness, the old bishop tells me of his vain efforts to find a "homestead" for his small community in Europe. He has approached various European governments, including German parliamentarians, with a request to take in the Qaraqosh exiles as a group and prevent them being scattered around the globe.

"I asked them to assign us a safe area where we could continue living as a community, in order to keep our language and culture alive. We need to be able to hope that peace, and above all, freedom, for non-Muslims will be restored to Iraq one day, so that we can return to our old homeland. And that would be so much easier if the people could preserve their family ties, their culture, and their language."

But Bishop Petros's request fell on deaf ears in Europe – ghettoization was not something to be encouraged. Such concerns are understandable, but the bishop wasn't seeking to establish a parallel society – all he wanted was to give

a small community the chance to preserve its heritage.
Nor would Aramaic Christians have any major problems
adapting to European culture. For one thing, they have
no religious rules governing food or women's dress, and
as Christians they are committed to monogamy and have
always placed a high value on education.

"My people are peace-loving and hard-working. We have
never taken up arms against anyone. And we have always
accepted and respected our Muslim neighbors, teaching
them in our schools and treating them in our hospitals
without discrimination. We Christians have made a great
contribution to the social development and culture of this
country. And now we are being driven away."

He heaves a loud sigh. "My parishioners are innocent
pawns in a game played out by political parties and superpowers seeking to assert their interests without regard for
the lives and dignity of those they affect."

Many people in Western countries, he points out,
campaign for the protection of animal species threatened
with extinction. And yet all appeals to halt the loss of the
oldest Christian culture and its people and language have
been ignored by the Western world.

I am reminded of the memorandum by the Society for
Threatened Peoples back in 2007, calling on the German
Chancellor Angela Merkel to grant the Christian settlement
area autonomous status and place it under international
protection, along with the multiethnic federal state of Kurdistan. It was, after all, the Eastern Christians who had paid
the highest price – in blood – for the failed policies of the
United States and its allies. Yet they were never compensated for their suffering.

Indeed, when has global politics ever paid any serious
attention to the Christian minority in Islamic states, or
made any moves to protect it? Which states have called

unequivocally for equal rights for Christians? Wasn't the
Aramaic Christian culture, where people still speak and
celebrate the liturgy in the native language of Jesus, worthy
of being declared part of our intangible world heritage?
And yet this world is disappearing before the indifferent
eyes of Western countries which claim to be committed to
human rights.

There is another question I want to ask Bishop Petros: "As
someone who has spent his whole life as a Christian in an
Islamic country, what is your view of Islam?"

"The vast majority of Muslims want to live in peace, go
about their work, and enjoy their children – just like most
other people. But Islam is in conflict with itself, and the
indigenous Christians, who have never been at war, are
being wiped out in the conflict. We lived in harmony with
our neighbors for many years. But our Muslim friends have
disappointed us deeply on a personal level. Some have even
supported the IS terrorists."

Frowning, the bishop poses some critical questions
of his own: "Those famous Islamic scholars who pipe up
at major international conferences, claiming that Islam
respects religious freedom and human rights and is a religion of peace: where were they when we were expelled, just
for being Christians? When will Muslim scholars under-
take a critical investigation of the roots of the violence
perpetrated in the name of Islam?"

He then quotes his colleague, Bishop Amel Shimon Nona,
who says that Islam, too, has a humanist potential, but
that it remains untapped because the faith has stood still
for centuries. Instead, radical fundamentalism is growing.
Bishop Nona reminds the West of a crucial point: "Islam
does not say that all men are equal. Your values are not their
values." Whether an enlightened Islam can emerge remains

to be seen. What is clear is that imams or intellectuals who advocate a modern Islam are a marginal phenomenon in Muslim countries and often face death threats.

At the same time, Islam benefits from European values and rights such as religious freedom and tolerance, which help it spread without having to adopt those same fundamental rights itself. Europe is under the illusion that the Muslim masses pouring into the continent are peaceable and tolerant. By contrast, Saudi Arabia and Qatar won't take any refugees even though they share the same religion, language, and culture – precisely because they fear unrest and terror. Bishop Petros adds: "The Saudis are smarter than your governments."

Glancing at the clock, the old man regrets that he must draw our conversation to a close. He gets up and bids me farewell with a deep sadness in his eyes: "Pray for us!"

Then he offers me a lift to the center of Ankawa; he has a meeting with the Slovak diplomatic mission about the reception of refugees from his community. He hands me a pack of papers to bring to the car for him. They are baptism certificates, signed by the bishop to confirm that the holders were baptized and belong to the Syriac Church. Now these documents are serving to save lives – if also to tear that church apart and scatter its members far and wide.

As we drive past the Yazidi camp, the bishop turns to me. "I think you might find it interesting to meet Claire. She's French by birth, and dedicates herself mainly to the interests of Yazidi women." He gives me her number, and when we get to Ankawa I give her a call. I'm in luck: she has time for me today. We arrange to meet in a nearby café.

While I am waiting, I reflect on my conversation with Bishop Petros. What impressed me most was his ability – despite all the injustices suffered by his people – not to think of revenge, but to hope for reconciliation. For me, this represents a core principle of Christianity.

Soon Claire arrives, wearing a knee-length dark blue dress with a beige sweater over the top. She looks about fifty, and works for a church relief organization. She is familiar with my community, and so a basis of trust is soon established between us. Claire tells me about her work in the refugee camps, and goes on to reveal her most harrowing experience. After the jihadists had taken the mainly Yazidi town of Sinjar, she tells me, they enslaved large numbers of women and girls.

....

Jesus of Nazareth proclaimed a father-like God who loves all people as his children. By his actions, Jesus showed that God's new world would begin when the sick are healed, the excluded assimilated, and the estranged reconciled. This new, universal brotherhood would also put an end once and for all to the use of violence between people. Jesus demonstrated through his words and example that the deadly cycle of violence can be broken by mercy and forgiveness, allowing a new peace to flourish.

Jesus was himself a victim of unjust violence, condemned to death by his fellow men. But God did not abandon him in death; rather, Jesus' message of nonviolence, reconciliation, and peace was vindicated for all time through his resurrection.

This opens up a new set of choices for us as human beings. No longer do we have to assert ourselves through violence; instead, we find ourselves free to love others, even our enemies. When Jesus preached this kind of love, he meant it less as an emotion and more in the sense of respecting our enemies' rights as fellow human beings.

....

To this day, one of the most senior Saudi clerics, Sheikh Fawzan, still justifies slavery as an element of Islam and jihad. And IS has proudly announced the reintroduction of slavery as part of the return to original Islam. From the beginning, jihadists were motivated not just by the prospect of paradise but also by distinctly earthly pleasures, such as the spoils of war and the use of female slaves for sexual gratification. "Unbelieving" women and girls are regarded as sex objects to which deserving IS warriors, according to their religious belief, have a right as reward for their service in the "holy war." Accordingly, as they swept through Iraq, IS fighters captured thousands of Yazidi and Christian children, young girls, and women and sold them on modern-day slave markets.

Several groups of abused women in Mosul and Sinjar managed to escape. Five hundred of them were taken in by Germany at the initiative of the Society for Threatened Peoples and given therapeutic support. Claire was invited to join a team of women appointed to prepare the Yazidi women for the journey to Germany. In their discussions, she heard the grim facts about what these women had undergone. In Mosul, Yazidi women were imprisoned in a confiscated Christian house where they were sorted into virgins, young married women, and older married women, and either priced and sold accordingly or placed at the disposal of the religious fighters.

Claire tells me, "One young woman told me in confidence that she was raped continuously for days on end by a dozen men, in every way imaginable. She was so exhausted that she begged the men to kill her, but they only laughed and made cynical remarks. They also beat her repeatedly. She burst into violent sobbing fits as she told me her story, and I had to hold her in my arms for a long time."

Another account was similarly horrifying: "The terrorists imprisoned all the young women from my village in a house. Suddenly I heard shots outside and looked out through a chink in the curtain. Our menfolk were being gunned down one by one. I cried out loud, and a female guard came at once, threatening to shoot us all if I made any more trouble."

Many women and girls take their own life out of shame after being raped, feeling their honor and dignity so violated that they can't go on living. To make matters worse, their own families sometimes regard rape as a disgrace that can never be effaced.

Claire speaks quietly, often with her eyes closed. I can see how much it pains her to recall these encounters, and indicate that she needn't go on – I do not need to know any more. But she takes a deep breath and continues, perhaps because she wants to get something off her chest by sharing it with someone.

"I've also met Christian girls who have been subjected to bestial abuse by jihadists. One of them was Raphid. I knew what had happened and visited her in the shack where she was living with her family. She didn't want to talk to me. Her face was haggard and her eyes vacant, as if her soul had been snuffed out. Her mother sat at the table crying; her father just stared into the distance. I was really worried about that girl, but I couldn't bring her back. The next day I heard that she'd taken rat poison, and arrived too late to save her. The convulsions lasted for hours; it was a terribly long, drawn-out death."

I lay a hand on Claire's arm, tears springing to my eyes.

She nods wordlessly. After a while she looks at me sadly. "You see, sometimes honor is so important to Christian families that they don't try to intervene."

I return home to Yousif's family, overwhelmed by my experiences. Wearily I clatter up the iron staircase to the apartment, where Taghrid, Basman, and Yousif are sitting drinking tea. I slump onto a couch, almost too tired to accept their offer to pour me a cup.

I tell them briefly about my encounters. There is one more question I want to ask.

"You're from Mosul. What do you know about your ancestors? When did they come to Mosul?"

Yousif points to his mother: "Her family has always lived in Mosul. Perhaps since the beginning of Christianity. But my paternal grandfather was a refugee."

I am curious to know more. "A refugee? From where?"

"From Siirt, which is now in Turkey."

"And when did he come to Mosul?"

"In 1915. Exactly a hundred years ago. He was twelve years old at the time."

"Do you know any more about his escape, and about what happened in Siirt?"

"I never knew my grandpa. My father learned a lot from hearing him talk about it." Yousif nods sadly. "But he's no longer around to ask."

We are silent for a while, looking at the floor. Then Yousif continues, "Uncle Jonah, he knows a lot too. He even has an old book that my grandpa wrote."

Galvanized by this news, I ask, "I'd love to see that. Do you think your uncle might be able to spare a bit of time?"

Yousif laughs wryly.

"The people here may have virtually nothing to their name, but if there's one thing they have in abundance, it's time. Ankawa is like one big waiting room. Uncle Jonah is glad of any distraction, particularly since the death of his wife two years ago. We'll pay him a visit tomorrow."

9

Nothing New under the Crescent Moon

Uncle Jonah lives in a low-cost housing block similar to Taghrid's, but with the luxury of a small front yard. As Yousif is obliged to spend another day under a car, Wadid takes me to see his brother, who has lunch ready for us when we arrive. Jonah is an extremely polite man and is highly gratified by my interest in his family's history.

He has even opened a bottle of red wine, proudly explaining that he managed to salvage a few precious items just before fleeing Mosul for Kurdistan: a couple of bottles of good-quality wine and a box of old books. We drink a toast to better times. After lunch, Jonah clears the table and goes to the cupboard to fetch another treasure rescued from Mosul: a handwritten book of his father's. He had been determined not to let the manuscript fall into the hands of the IS terrorists, who would doubtless have burned it. Carefully, Jonah opens the precious heirloom. I am fascinated by the clear, neat handwriting, but am unable to identify it. It can't be Arabic, but looks similar.

Wadid reads my mind. "It's Syriac – or Aramaic. It's the same thing."

I turn the pages reverently. The accurately formed letters remind me of biblical manuscripts preserved in European monasteries. Jonah lets me take a few photos.

"What's it about?" I ask.

"It's from the Bible – my father copied out large sections of it."

I continue turning the pages excitedly, but am a little disappointed. I was hoping Yousif's grandfather might have kept some kind of diary or memoir.

"What did your father tell you?"

Jonah pulls out a few more books. Not handwritten ones, but books with illustrations and maps, through which the two brothers are able to relate the story of their family and people, books with titles such as *The Assyrians: The Oldest Christian People* and *The Hakkari Massacres* and *The Forgotten Genocide.*

Yousif's grandfather's hometown, Siirt, is in Eastern Anatolia, then Western Armenia, which had a large Christian population. Most of the Christians were Armenians who were slaughtered or deported during the genocide of 1915. The ethnic cleansing policies of the "Young Turk" government not only affected Armenians, however, but also the substantial Greek minority, along with Aramaic Christians. Around 1900, about 20 percent of those living in the area now known as Turkey were Christian. But it wasn't long before the national mania to create an exclusively Turkish state led to the first genocide of the twentieth century. The First World War kept public attention well away from what was going on in the remoter regions of the Ottoman Empire. Overshadowed by the atrocities committed against the Greeks (approximately 350,000 dead) and Armenians (approximately 1.5 million dead), the genocide of around 300,000 Aramaic Christians has barely registered in the global consciousness to this day.

The motives for the genocide were complex. In the First World War, the Ottoman Empire fought against

(Christian) Russia in the Caucasus and regarded its own native Christians as potential enemy collaborators. This was compounded by Turkish nationalism, with influential politicians referring to Christians as "germs," "viruses," and "internal tumors" that had colonized the body of the Turkish nation and needed to be combated and eradicated. Material greed also played a major part, as Christian houses and businesses were now up for grabs. At the same time, the high value that Christians placed on education led to envy and jealousy among the less educated Turks.

But the 1915 genocide was not just politically or socially motivated. Religion, too, was a key factor, as is clear from the alternatives placed before Armenian or Aramaic Christians. They could convert to Islam and keep all their possessions, or be murdered.

There are numerous documents testifying to the prominent role of religiously motivated contempt for Christians in the unspeakable brutality of the massacre. This hostility is rooted in the systematic discrimination against Christians in the Muslim world which has time and time again erupted openly in carnage.

Already in 1843, thousands of Aramaic Christians had been horrifically slaughtered by Kurds in an area to the north of Mosul. The women and girls left behind were abducted and forced to convert to Islam; those who protested were burned. Eduard Sachau, a German scholar of the Middle East, wrote at the time, "The Kurds have shed Christian blood in such streams that one could run a mill with it."

Again, in the anti-Christian pogroms of 1894–96, imams incited Muslims to violence at the command of the notorious "Bloody Sultan" Abdulhamid II (1842–1918); in total, some fifty thousand Aramaic Christians were killed and around a hundred thousand forced to adopt Islam.

Then, in 1915, the biggest and bloodiest persecution of Aramaic Christians was organized systematically by the Ottoman government in a bid to implement a "final solution" to the problem of Christians on Turkish soil. Once again, the choice was one of expulsion or death, or conversion to Islam. According to one account, an entire group of Christians sang sacred songs as they confronted their fate. They were made to kneel down, one after another, and a knife was held to their throats with the words, "Embrace Islam – or die!" As none were willing to renounce their Christian faith, every single throat was cut. In total, over two million Christians were killed for their beliefs, while hundreds of thousands were forced by fire and sword to convert to Islam.

I sit silently, poring over the historic photos in Uncle Jonah's books. The emaciated bodies of children, the piled-up corpses, the hanged and mutilated victims – all these images remind me of the documentation I have seen of the Shoah or Holocaust, the persecution of the Jews in the Third Reich. I learn that the use of the term holocaust (meaning "a whole burnt offering") to denote the destruction of human beings dates back to the burning of Christians in the Ottoman Empire. In the pogroms of 1895, Armenian Christians sought sanctuary in the cathedral of Urfa, whereupon the Turks barricaded them in to prevent their escape before setting fire to the building. Forced to witness the burning alive of at least three thousand men, women, and children, the American missionary Corinna Shattuck branded this mass murder a "holocaust." In 1915, the Turks deployed the "methods of the holocaust" systematically in order to

destroy Christians in Turkey. It wasn't until 1955 that the
term "holocaust" was applied to the extermination of Jews
by the Nazis.

"So what exactly happened in Siirt in 1915?" I ask Uncle
Jonah.

"My father had six siblings, and had left them behind
for a few days in order to accompany my grandfather on a
visit to relatives in a nearby village. When they returned,
the Turkish massacre of Christians was already raging.
My grandfather was recognized by a Muslim neighbor and
beheaded before the eyes of his twelve-year-old son. Then
they cut off his arms and legs and threw them into the
street for dogs and rats to feed on."

There is a brief, oppressive silence in the room. Then
Wadid continues, "My father often told me how he cried
out in fear and tried to run away. But he was seized and
dragged to the square in front of the cathedral, where lots of
Aramaic women and children were being rounded up. They
were to be resettled and had hastily thrown together a few
belongings. He found his aunt and asked where his mother
was. She had already been stabbed to death along with her
other six children."

The Turkish forces and their Kurdish auxiliaries invariably
used the same strategy when raiding the many Christian towns and villages. First, they would round up all
the able-bodied men. Some would be put in chains and
made to work on projects such as the Baghdad railway
(an industrial project supported by the German Empire),
only to be bayoneted to death when the job was finished.
The other men were taken out of the villages or towns
and immediately shot or beheaded. Then the women and

children were seized and gathered together to be sent on
death marches – officially known as "resettlements" – to the
Mesopotamian desert. Anyone who resisted was killed on
the spot. Most of the sick or elderly Christians died within
the first few days of the marches. In the villages along the
way, the deportees were often robbed, so that they ended
up virtually naked. Local men preyed on the women and
girls, raping them in broad daylight or singling out the most
attractive and dragging them off to their harems. Many of
the young Christian boys were circumcised and placed in
Muslim families. The majority of the women and children
perished cruelly from exhaustion, hunger, or thirst during
the long march. The column of shriveled figures driven
mercilessly onward by the Turkish soldiers was trailed in
the sky by vultures and followed on the road by a pack of
dogs, fighting over every new corpse.

Uncle Jonah's books contain accounts of the deportations
that are almost unbearable:

"When night fell, the militias came to where we were
sleeping in the open and shone a match in every face,
looking for pretty girls. After they had abused them, they
handed them over to the Kurds to be killed."

"Some Kurds escorting us on the next stage of the
journey suddenly pounced on two or three young girls who
were with us and raped them in front of our eyes. We were
left naked and exposed."

"My glance fell on a completely naked woman who had
been stabbed with a dagger. She was bleeding heavily and
trying to hold in her bulging guts with her hands."

I can hardly bring myself to look at the reports. But Uncle
Wadid is not through. In one of the books, he shows me a
passage describing the bloodbath in Siirt, where the bishop
of the city and all the priests of his diocese were killed along

with their flock. The city's Turks rejoiced at the fact that all Christians in Siirt had now been destroyed or expelled, and the mullahs (Islamic clerics) who had participated in the slaughter declared that, from now on, any Christian daring to return to the city would be killed on the spot.

The cathedral of Siirt was turned into a barn and its famous library reduced to ashes. All the headstones in the Christian cemetery were smashed and the graves defiled with excrement. The nuns at the convent were also deported, and their abbess, who was too old to join the march, was nailed to a cross. The sixteen sisters sang litanies on their exodus from the city, determined not to let all the atrocities stop them proclaiming their Christian faith. On the way, a number of girls from Siirt threw themselves into a river, preferring to drown rather than be raped on the march.

After a long silence, Wadid returns to his father's story. "Out of the thousands of Christians from Siirt, only about a hundred survived the massacres and death marches. When the trail of deportees arrived in Mosul, their feet bloody with blisters, my father was just skin and bone. But he was still alive, and was taken in by an orphanage."

With a penetrating look, Uncle Wadid whispers, "1915. And exactly a hundred years later the same thing is happening again – the exodus of an entire people, murder and rape, then a steady decline as they languish in refugee camps."

"The exodus of an entire people," I repeat. "Qaraqosh and the Nineveh Plain."

"And back then Western Armenia, Tur Abdin, and the Hakkari mountains too. Have you ever heard of the mountain Assyrians?"

I have to confess that I haven't.

Wadid starts to tell me their story and I hang on every word, aghast at what I am hearing.

The Syriac Church continued to flourish from Persia to the Mediterranean until the thirteenth century, when the Mongol hordes murdered hundreds of thousands of Christians, burned down cities, churches, and monasteries and virtually wiped out Christianity in the East. The only surviving Christian populations were in mountainous regions like those of Lebanon or Tur Abdin. One example was the Hakkari mountains, an Alp-like territory to the north of Mosul. There, the Christian mountain Assyrians maintained a relatively autonomous existence under the leadership of a patriarch, with organized defenses to protect their villages and livestock from marauding Kurdish tribes.

On February 4, 1916, the *Frankfurter Zeitung* published an appeal for help by the patriarch: "When the constitution was introduced in Turkey, we believed the government's promises to guarantee our security, and sold the majority of our weapons on the assurance that the Kurds had been similarly disarmed. As a result, our people were left defenseless. After the declaration of jihad, the Turks decided to exterminate us along with the Armenians, and sent in their troops to attack us, aided by the Kurds among whom we lived. At the end of May, Turkish troops from Mosul invaded our territory. That was when the official massacres and devastation of our villages began."

The patriarch's appeal in the German press was to no avail. The entire tribe of mountain Assyrians were forced to leave their age-old churches and monasteries and flee the mountains for the Urmia Plain in Persia. There, they hoped for protection from the Russians, with whom they had meanwhile formed an alliance. This exodus of an entire people saw around half of the original 160,000 Christians killed by slaughter, epidemics, and starvation. The corpses were left lying around, denied a burial, due to the Muslim contempt of Christian "impurity."

Further harrowing accounts follow: "One of the most abominable things that came to the knowledge of the medical department [of the US Presbyterian mission in Urmia] was the treatment of women and girls, who had been violated by the Turks, Kurds, and local Muslims. After the massacre in the village of N., all women and girls were raped; two girls aged eight and ten died at the hands of these Muslim brutes. One mother reported that no girl above the age of twelve escaped this violation. One man of some influence in the north of the Urmia Plain boasted that he had raped eleven Christian girls, two of them under the age of seven."

Wadid opens another book and I scan a passage highlighting the active involvement of the Muslim population in this butchery; only in rare cases did Muslims give shelter to persecuted Christians, many of them fearing that the contact would render them "impure." By contrast, Jewish and Yazidi families were often ready to help.

Appalled, I stare at the open books containing the reports from 1915. This isn't just something that happened a hundred years ago and a thousand miles away: today, in 2015, a mere twenty miles from here, Christians are once again being shot, beheaded, or crucified – purely for being Christian. The archive photographs in the books are grisly enough; today, online videos show Christians being beheaded with a cry of "Allahu akbar!" or crucified victims surrounded by gawking, jeering crowds. Their bodies are mutilated and thrown to the dogs. Incited by imams, Muslims loot the houses of Christians and set fire to their churches. Islamists rape women and girls and treat them as sex slaves. I think back on my conversations with Claire and with Bishop Petros Mouche, whose concern for the missing girls keeps him awake at night.

I have one more question for Jonah: "What happened to the mountain Assyrians after they fled?"

"Ah, it's a sad story, nor did it have a happy ending, I'm afraid. After the revolution of 1917, the Russians abandoned the Assyrians. That led to further massacres, so the survivors were forced to flee Urmia again and head further south. They ended up in refugee camps and spent years being shunted from pillar to post."

The migrants, Jonah tells me, were keen to go back to their homeland after the First World War, but the victorious powers took no interest in the fate of this small tribe, and the Turks violently blocked their return. Their villages were occupied by Kurds; the churches, some of them dating back to the fourth century, were destroyed or used as mosques; the old monasteries with their priceless manuscripts were burned down. Today, not a single Christian remains in this seat of early Christianity. The survivors in the refugee camps became a mere plaything of the colonial powers. In the hope that Britain would support their bid to return to their native territory, Assyrians volunteered for service in the British army. But after the British withdrawal the refugees, far from getting their promised settlement zone, bore the brunt of the new Arab rulers' hatred. In 1933, there were more mass murders in the Plain of Mosul, this time perpetrated by the Iraqi army. Once again, young men who refused to convert to Islam were shot and women raped. Pregnant women had their bellies slashed open and infants were crushed under heavy vehicles. Babies were thrown into the air and speared on bayonets.

After blaming each other for this catastrophe, France and Britain eventually conceived a plan to settle the mountain Assyrians in Timbuktu, British Guyana, or Brazil. In the end, though, the Hakkari Christians found refuge in Syria and settled in thirty-four villages along the Khabur

River. They called their villages "camps" as they were, strictly speaking, refugee camps, and the inhabitants still cherished the hope of returning to their homeland one day. But at least they could live in relative freedom in Syria, like the Arameans in the nearby cities of Hassake and Qamishli – that is, until the IS "holy warriors" arrived on the scene in 2015 and the attacks and abductions began all over again. Over two hundred abducted Christians are still being held to date, including thirty-nine children under the age of ten. Exactly a hundred years after their exodus, the mountain Assyrians found themselves on the move once more – this time to Europe, Australia, and America. "If we are forced to emigrate again, we'll have to go to the moon," one Aramaic Christian told a German newspaper. But does this small tribe have any realistic hope of survival? Dispersed around the globe, its culture, language, and Christian tradition look set to be erased forever.

I feel rather queasy inside as Jonah empties the wine bottle and we drink once again "to a better future!" He gazes meditatively into the distance: "Perhaps humans will learn from history one day . . ."

Then Jonah gets up, goes over to one of the shelves, and plucks out a paperback. "This is by Bishop Saliba, whom you saw in church on Sunday. He translated an eleventh-century encyclopedia from Aramaic into Arabic."

"A bishop and a translator?"

"Yes, he was originally a monk. In our Eastern churches it's traditional for monks to be appointed as bishops."

"Does he belong to a monastery?"

"Yes, to a famous one, in fact: Mar Mattai."

"Is it open to visitors?"

Wadid frowns. "Hmmm, it's right near the front between the peshmerga and the Islamic State."

I can't help feeling disappointed; I would love to have visited such an old and renowned Syriac monastery. I feel a strange attraction to this place, almost like wanting to take a last look at a disappearing land before it sinks into the sea – or a coffin before it is covered with earth.

Back at home with Yousif's family, the TV is on as it is every evening and, like every evening, the living room is turned into a theater of war, with exploding bombs, machine gun fire, and rolling tanks – in Iraq, Syria, Yemen, Palestine, Lebanon, and Libya. Between two reports comes a commercial for the peshmerga: good-looking young men in combat uniform present arms over a pop soundtrack, followed by images of tanks firing grenades, rocket launchers in full swing, soldiers storming buildings, and finally another dashing soldier singing the refrain "peshmerga, peshmerga!" I am haunted by the ugly thought that this commercial may have been sponsored by the German weapon manufacturers who are arming the peshmerga forces.

One news item in particular makes us sit up and take note. Today, Thursday, November 12, 2015, peshmerga and Yazidi troops have managed to drive the IS fighters out of Sinjar. This city and the nearby mountains form the center of the proverbially peaceable Yazidi population which has suffered so persistently under IS. In an interview, someone is saying that Mosul will be next to be freed from the clutches of IS. Yousif's family stares mutely at the screen. Yesterday evening, his mother showed me a bunch of keys. Dare she dream of getting her home back one day? The IS militants have probably long since broken down the doors and taken possession of the house, looting and vandalizing all its contents. Is there still a ray of hope?

10

············

Within Sight of the Islamic State

My last day in Ankawa. Uncle Wadid has invited me on
another excursion, although our destination remains curiously uncertain. Mar Mattai being out of bounds, I had
inquired the evening before whether there were any other
old churches or early Christian monasteries in Kurdistan.
After some conferring, Yousif and Wadid come up with
one. Now I am feeling a little on edge, not knowing quite
what to expect.

We are accompanied by Aunt Fadia and the couple's
two daughters, Janet and Wasan, who don't have school on
Fridays. We eat breakfast at six thirty while Fadia prepares a
delicious picnic, frying chicken cutlets, chopping vegetables,
and packing bread and cheese into a big bag. The air outside
smells invigoratingly fresh after the rain of the last few days,
and the morning breaks to reveal a cloudless, deep blue sky.
We drive across Erbil, which shows its best face, resplendent
with lavishly planted verges. The road, on the other hand,
offers a few nasty surprises in the shape of large potholes
and unexpected speed bumps. Not that these do anything
to curb Uncle Wadid's speed mania; with his car licked back
into shape by Yousif, Wadid overtakes with abandon, apparently deaf to the shrieks from the back seat.

Soon, oil installations begin to appear on the horizon,
with immense tanks beside them and gas flames burning

above the tall stacks. I wonder what the Arab countries would look like today had oil not been discovered: no interference from Western colonial powers; no billions upon billions of petrodollars for the Islamist arms build-up. What course would modern Islam have taken without the vast sums of money pumped into the construction of mosques and the recruitment of Salafists from around the world? Was the black gold really a blessing for the Gulf States and their inhabitants? How many battles have been fought in this region over access to the oil wells – in the two World Wars, the Gulf Wars, and to this day?

The two girls and their mother start singing hymns from the Syriac liturgy in Aramaic. We are heading west, and from the road signs I gather that we are approaching Mosul. Then the barricades and checkpoints begin. Uncle Wadid slows down a long way ahead, and we creep toward the barriers. Behind piles of sandbags a metal hut glints in the sun, a tattered Kurdish flag flying above it. A few very young peshmerga fighters lean against a wall, brandishing their Kalashnikovs. Wadid stops and winds down the window. He says a few words in Kurdish and points to the rosary beads dangling from the rearview mirror. We are waved through; clearly, Christians are not perceived as a threat.

From here we head north, toward the Turkish border. We pass the occasional small village. The houses are low-rise blocks scattered randomly into the landscape like dice, some white and terracotta-colored, some pink and blue. Here and there, a minaret rises between the jumble of houses, slender and pointed like a pencil. The plain gives way to a gently undulating landscape. "Now it's all brown and dry," explains Wadid, "but in the spring this land is fresh and green. Huge areas are planted with wheat." I picture a wavy green carpet covering the wide expanse.

We reach another junction with checkpoints, and I hear
Fadia talking on the phone in the back. At a fork in the road,
Fadia and Wadid exchange a few words.

"We've decided where we're going," Wadid explains to
me with a broad smile. He won't say any more, and I don't
want to dash my hopes by speaking too soon. Soon a mountain ridge appears on the horizon, standing out for miles
from the otherwise monotonously flat landscape: we are
approaching Jebel Maklub.

At last the secret is out: we are going to Mar Mattai after
all – the early Christian monastery with which Yousif's
family has been closely connected for generations. Fadia's
phone call had been to a monk at the monastery, to check
on the current security situation. Now I am more agitated
than ever. I am touched by Yousif's family's desire to grant
my wish to visit an ancient monastery, but I can't help
feeling a slight palpitation, given IS's notorious propensity
for surprise attacks. I think of Janet and Wasan on the back
seat. But the excursion would have been virtually impossible
without the girls, Wadid explains to me later. Two men traveling alone are far more likely to arouse suspicion, especially
if one has an Iraqi and the other a German passport. Not
long ago, a German jihadist, Abu Osama al Almani, plowed
into a peshmerga checkpoint with a car full of explosives,
killing himself and taking twenty Kurds with him.

We pass another checkpoint, then another. We are
getting close to the front now. The rosary beads on the
mirror serve as a badge of safe conduct. Above all, however,
the presence of a wife and two children on the back seat
lend credibility to Wadid's explanation: we are a Christian
family displaced from Mosul, taking advantage of the day of
rest to enjoy an outing to Mar Mattai Monastery.

A peshmerga truck overtakes us, juddering along
the potholed road. The gun mounted on the truck bed

is pointing directly at us. I remember that Germany is
currently supplying the peshmerga with weapons and
the German military is training its units; I can only hope
they've already been trained how to keep a gun from going
off accidentally in bumpy conditions. This hair-raising
situation continues for a while until the Kurdish fighters
finally turn off the road. I let out a sigh of relief.

A little later, Uncle Wadid points to a sandstone-colored
patch among the craggy mountains and I spot the imposing
monastery complex, nestling high up in a steep rocky landscape. An elaborately laid, wide footpath snakes upward
from the foot of the mountain, but there is now vehicle
access too via a serpentine road built some years ago. As
Uncle Wadid powers around the bends, the whole family
starts singing from the Syriac liturgy again. A road sign
indicates that Mosul is just over twenty miles away. Wadid
recalls that Mar Mattai was a popular destination for many
Christians from the city – a place of pilgrimage in a breath-
taking setting, where Aramaic Christians could be sure of a
warm welcome.

We too are greeted warmly by one of the monks. Then,
on a bench by the church entrance, I spot Bishop Saliba in a
black habit and red cap, absorbed in solemn contemplation.
I try to read the venerable, wrinkled face and think how
painful it must be for this elderly, erudite monk to see the
last remnants of his church disappear. Catching sight of
Wadid's family, he welcomes us with open arms.

We pass through courtyards separated by arcades and
climb up to sweeping terraces with spectacular views.
Huddled in the plain below are a few Christian villages,
now largely deserted – a reminder that IS rule begins
directly behind the next hill. I strain my eyes but can't
make out anything unusual.

"At night," Wadid informs me, "the militia scans the whole area with its searchlight."

I realize that we must have driven to within less than half a mile of an IS checkpoint; my stomach churns at the thought. I hear a canary singing its heart out from the belfry. The atmosphere up here breathes tranquility. It's a strange feeling – an oasis of peace within sight of a territory dominated by war and terror.

There are two other families here besides us. The place used to be overrun with people on vacation days, I am told. In the summer months, Christians would flock here to escape the stifling heat of Mosul and enjoy the fresh evening breeze on these wide open terraces. The last time there was a large crowd up here was sixteen months ago, in June 2014 – only on that occasion it wasn't the summer breeze they were seeking, but a safe haven. Many of the Christian families displaced from Mosul found refuge in Mar Mattai. The monastery was soon bursting at the seams. Hundreds of people slept on the terraces and cooked together on the canteen gas cookers. For two months they lived like one big family – until the religious fighters began to advance on the monastery and the refugees were forced to take flight again, this time in the direction of Ankawa or Duhok.

In a dome above the richly decorated monastery portal hangs a bell that Yousif's father and his brothers restored and installed. I take off my shoes and put them in the rack by the entrance before stepping onto the carpeted floor of the church. The altar is hidden behind a curtain; in front of it stands a lectern bearing the Book of the Gospels, which we kiss in turn with a deep bow. We sit on a pew and remain for a while in silent prayer. It's a typically Syriac church, with hardly any pictures. Above the altar hangs a wooden cross with rounded ends like a three-leaved clover – a symbol of the Trinity. Syriac crosses never depict a crucified figure, but are always bare, signifying that death does not have the last word. Jesus Christ, who suffered unjustly and prayed for his antagonists with his dying breath, was resurrected by God. For a church which has seen so much hardship and suffering since its inception, the cross is a symbol of hope: people who suffer unjustly yet continue to love can hope that their suffering will not be in vain, and that their love will endure.

In a side room, we visit the burial niche of Mar Mattai. This saint, named after the evangelist Matthew, came from Amida (now Diyarbakir in Turkey). He left his wealthy family and came to this wild mountain landscape to live as a hermit. From an inscription I learn that in the year 344 (more than 150 years before Benedict of Nursia), Mattai founded a community of monks, which has prayed, celebrated the liturgy, and taken in guests on this site for over sixteen hundred years. One of the Christian villages in the valley is named Alfaf, the Arabic word for "thousand" – a reminder that a thousand monks once prayed and worked here. Syriac monasteries were traditionally places of learning; Mar Mattai houses a rich library of rare manuscripts.

Above all, the monasteries were places of tranquility, prayer, and meditation. The same was true of the hermitages built into the rock face. Wadid beckons to me and we clamber up – somewhat adventurously – to a cave concealed in the rock and closed off with a wooden door. This hermitage appears to be in use.

Regular retreats to a hermitage are part of the spiritual life of my community, the Little Brothers. We cultivate silence in order to retreat into our inner selves. Standing next to the cave, I feel a spiritual connection with this great monastic tradition of seeking God in a place of silence and solitude. As Augustine wrote, if you want to find God, you shouldn't go out into the external world. "Return into your-self, for truth dwells in the inner being." To experience God, we need to stop and take a break from the bustle of worldly activity. In periods of solitude, I have sometimes been blessed with a sense that, in my innermost being, I am not alone, but close to God. I am able to refocus on what really matters to me deep down. Sometimes this has helped me reconcile myself to past injuries I had previously suppressed, finally giving them a chance to heal in silence.

I sit on a rock for a moment, looking into the distance. Overwhelmed by the impressions of the last few days, I am keen to put them into a prayer, so that I can review them calmly before God and place all the unresolved painful and disturbing matters in his hands. If only I could stay here longer . . .

But Yousif's uncle has already moved on, and is pointing out some cliffs in a side valley. They are riddled with aban-doned caves, giving me a sense of the many hermits who have inhabited this barren mountain landscape. I follow Wadid over the scree and down into a valley where he shows me the monastery's water supply. In the old days, the monks had to carry water up the formidable winding path with the aid of donkeys – until Wadid's father donated a pump and installed a pipeline a few decades ago.

A rumble of artillery sounds in the distance. "Now you can hear IS," Wadid says. We return to the monastery and take a moment to admire the panorama once more before enjoying our picnic. At the exit, we come across an aban-doned building. This was to have been a seminary for young monks, but since the expulsion of the Mosul Christians it has remained an empty shell, likely never to be completed. Where would new recruits come from now? The abbot and the younger monk are sitting on the viewing platform and gazing toward Mosul, where the IS fighters rule by terror and violence. Could these three monks of Mar Mattai, seeking God in this silent, peaceful spot, be the last of a dying breed here in Iraq?

If I am not mistaken, Mar Mattai is the only one of Iraq's ancient monasteries where the tradition of Eastern monasticism is still alive. Many were destroyed in persistent attacks – by Persians, Arabs, Mongols, Turks, and Kurds. Monks were massacred and invaluable manuscripts consumed by fire. Today, IS continues that destruction. The modern incarnation of Muslim fanaticism goes as far as to blow up the ruins and raze them to the ground in order to efface all reminders of Islam's Jewish and Christian roots.

One by one, the many monasteries of Mesopotamia – those seats of learning and culture – have been reduced to ashes and rubble. Seen by night from a bird's eye perspective, this would be like watching a series of lights go out one by one – a countdown from *hundreds* of monasteries all the way down to...

Three: The famous Rabban Hormizd Monastery, clinging to the rock face like an eagle's nest. In 1850, the building was looted by Kurds and its important collection of manuscripts was lost forever. During the Iraqi army crackdown on Kurdish rebels in 1969, the monastery was ransacked again following a massacre of unarmed monks and Christian civilians.

Two: The Monastery of Mar Behnam and Mart Sarah to the southeast of Mosul was occupied and ravaged by IS warriors in 2014. The monks were driven out and another collection of fifteen-hundred-year-old manuscripts went up in flames.

One: Mar Mattai. IS Islamists have advanced to within about two miles of the monastery as the crow flies. So far, it remains standing. But even if IS is defeated, other extremist Islamic groups will continue to proliferate. And the "monastery hinterland" – the Christian towns and villages from which young monks might otherwise have been recruited – has been deserted for the last year and a half, thus extinguishing one of the last potential sources of Iraqi monasticism.

11

The Decline of the Christian Middle East

Here at Mar Mattai, I can't stop thinking about the fate of the Syriac Christians. It's a strange feeling, like getting to know someone only to lose them again in an instant. I can reach out and touch a last rivulet of the great river of Eastern Christian history, only to see it seep into the sand before my eyes and disappear – perhaps forever. I am at the end of a fascinating story, looking back.

After Jesus' death, his disciples were overwhelmed by a powerful experience: God's resurrection of his crucified Son from the dead. The witnesses of the Easter morning miracle hastened to bring their hope to the rest of the world and proclaim it in every language. This mission is recorded in the Acts of the Apostles. The message of the gospel is proclaimed to the Romans and the inhabitants of the Greek provinces, and from there to those of Egypt and Libya, as far as Cyrene. The first to be named, however, are the Parthians, Medes, and Elamites – residents of Mesopotamia (Acts 2:9–11).

In other words, Christianity was disseminated across three continents from the outset. This is symbolized by three apostles: Paul took the gospel to the West, with its

Greco-Roman culture; Mark evangelized Alexandria and therefore stands for the church of (North) Africa; and the great missionary Thomas ventured into Asia, perhaps as far as India.

The trade routes had always doubled as communication channels, and Christianity spread rapidly along the major routes from Damascus via Palmyra and eastward to Mari, Arbela, and Basra. The legendary Silk Road extended continuously from Antioch to the Far East via Bukhara, Merv, and Samarkand. The first Christians, many of whom had Jewish roots, found a foothold for their mission in the far-flung Jewish communities of Mesopotamia. Paul is also known to have followed in the wake of Judaism on his missionary journeys, always preaching first in the synagogues, in Iconium, Athens, and Thessalonica. While Paul's letters to his community were preserved, those of the eastern-bound apostles have not survived. Consequently, few people know that early Christianity took hold not only in Ephesus, Corinth, and Rome, but also in Nisibis, Seleucia-Ctesiphon, and Gondeshapur.

....

Due to changing political boundaries, two **Syriac churches** evolved: a western one within the Roman Empire and an eastern one within the Persian domain (Parthians, Sassanids).

The church within the bounds of the Roman/Byzantine Empire styled itself the Syriac Church and its patriarch was based in the important city of Antioch. It was here that Jesus' disciples first were called "Christians" (Acts 11:26) and their place of worship was named "church" (kyriakon). Today, this church is known as the Syrian Orthodox Church.

The center of the Apostolic Church of the East (also known as the Persian Church, or Church of the East) was initially located in Seleucia-Ctesiphon (on the Tigris), and later in Baghdad. After Christianity was established as the state religion of the Roman Empire, Christians in the Persian domain began to be brutally persecuted, being suspected by the Persians of collaborating with the Roman enemy.

As a result of the political split, the Church of Antioch and the Church of the East went their separate ways, a fact reflected in their theological evolution. But their common language and culture have remained, to this day, a unifying element between two churches that have yielded a rich heritage in terms of their spirituality, liturgy, and scholarship.

Changes in the political boundaries (mainly due to the advance of Islamic Arabs) led to an overlap between the domains of the two churches, which later moved even further apart. Where the term "Syriac churches" is used in the following, it is understood to include all denominations characterized by the Aramaic language and Syriac culture. Where a particular denomination is meant, it is referred to explicitly.

Aramaic was the everyday language of Palestine, the Roman province of Syria, and Mesopotamia; this became the language of Syriac Christianity, which experienced a long and significant golden age. Monks from ancient Syria founded monasteries and hermitages as far west as Italy – a tradition which Benedict of Nursia drew on in order to found Western monasticism, which has shaped the culture of Western Europe for centuries. Indeed, several Syrians were appointed popes of Rome during the seventh and eighth centuries.

Christian monasticism flourished in the deserts and remote mountains of the Middle East. For centuries, this way of life exerted a remarkable pull, with thousands of men and women retreating into solitude. There, they cultivated silence and contemplative prayer, such as the "Jesus Prayer" – a mantra-like repetition of Jesus' name.

The churches in the cities and monasteries were lavishly decorated and – filled with the sublime chants of the Syriac liturgy – were meant to give the faithful a foretaste of heaven. Ephrem the Syrian (303–373), a great scholar of the early church famous for his writings and hymns, is credited with the introduction of female choirs. While the Latin West continued to exclude women from participation in the liturgy for a long time to come, he gave women an established place in the Christian ceremony by writing a number of hymns especially for female voices.

The Church of the East lived up to its name, spreading via merchants and monks as far as China and Siberia, India and the Philippines. There were bishoprics and monasteries in Kabul and Peking. At no time in its history did this church become a state religion; it never waged war, and it evangelized with passion, not force. Its missionaries came into contact with all kinds of cultures and engaged in a fruitful dialogue with them, as when Christian monks helped Indian Buddhists translate their sutras into Chinese – a collaboration strikingly symbolized by the cross on the lotus. Over centuries, this church has typically sought contact with other religions and preached the gospel by linking into their values. Foremost among the spiritual centers of Eastern Christianity were Edessa, Nisibis (now Nusaybin), and Gundeshapur, where Greco-Roman and Persian academic culture were preserved and disseminated.

The importance of Islamic philosophy in bringing ancient learning and thought to Western Europe is justly celebrated. At the same time, however, the instrumental role of Aramaic Christians in this process is unjustly ignored. Syriac monastic schools taught the works of Aristotle, and Christian academics passed on Greek philosophy and ancient scholarship to their Islamic colleagues. Over a millennium, Syriac Christianity produced scholars who paved the way for Islamic science. In Baghdad, for example, the legendary caliph Harun-al-Rashid commissioned the learned Christian patriarch Timotheus to translate Aristotle's *Topics* into Arabic, while the Christian physician and philosopher Hunayn ibn Ishaq translated more than a hundred ancient scripts into Syriac and thirty into Arabic. Paul the Persian, George, Bishop of the Arabs, and many other Christian philosophers laid the foundations for Islamic philosophy. The Syrians were particularly notable for their dynamic culture of philosophical teaching, which they handed down to Muslims. Baghdad's "House of Wisdom" continued the tradition of the Christian Academy of Gundeshapur, recruiting many of its staff from the Academy. Besides philosophy, Syrian academics also studied astronomy, mathematics, medicine, music, and optics; Gundeshapur housed the oldest known teaching hospital. In fact, it was Aramaic Christians who first adopted the Indian numeral system we now know as Arabic, long before it became widespread among Muslim scholars.

The Syriac churches had existed under Arab Muslim supremacy since the seventh century. At first, the Arab rulers treated Christians with considerable tolerance. This was partly for political reasons, to avoid provoking rebellion. After all, Christians had formed the majority of the Muslim-ruled Syrian population for centuries. And though superior in the art of war, Arabs were dependent on Christians for administration, trade, architecture, medicine, and science. At that time, many Christians converted voluntarily to Islam, which was in many ways similar to Syriac Christianity in its early days.

In the "Islamic Golden Age" (under the rule of the Abbasids, from the eighth to the thirteenth century), Christian, Jewish, and Muslim scholars alike presided over a flowering of philosophy and science. Equality prevailed in philosophical debate – but not in everyday life. Here, Christians found themselves under increasing social pressure as Muslim rule became more entrenched. As "protected peoples," they were, like Jews, tolerated as followers of a "book religion"; but, as the term "protected" suggests, their social status was problematic and required them to pay "protection money" in return for freedom to exercise their religion. For long periods, the *jizya* (poll tax) was the Islamic rulers' main source of income. Some tribes had to surrender half their property if they wanted to remain Christian. Those unable to bear the tax burden had no choice but to convert to Islam; otherwise their children would be sold into slavery. In the long term, the tax thus proved an effective instrument of enforced Islamization.

As "protected peoples," Christians naturally had a lower social status than their "protectors." For example, a Christian's testimony in court was worth less than that of a Muslim. The superiority of Islam and the inferiority of non-Muslims had to be publicly visible, so Christians and Jews were made to identify themselves via their clothing. The concept of the Jewish badge used in Europe has its origins in this Muslim act of discrimination. Under the Pact of Umar, concluded early on in Islam's history, Christians were forbidden to build any new monasteries or churches. Later they also had to forfeit the right to land ownership and the public exercise of their religion (for example, churches were forbidden to ring their bells).

The educated Christian class came under increasing pressure as the legislative course was set for the long-term Islamization of the entire population. Some occupations and higher-ranking positions in government and society were reserved exclusively for Muslims. Conversely, conversion to Islam became a passport to the club, opening the door to social advancement. Renunciation of one's Christian faith was always richly rewarded by Muslim rulers.

In a society where honor was accorded so much importance, Christians were subjected to systematic humiliations, such as not being allowed to ride horses, but only mules – and then only with a wooden saddle. The Islamization process was also boosted considerably by the marriage regulation whereby a Muslim woman could never marry a Christian man, but a Muslim man could marry a Christian woman, and their offspring were automatically deemed to be Muslim.

While Christians had been treated with respect in Islam's infancy, a growing polemic against Christianity emerged from the ninth century onward. Verbal attacks often led to violence, and again and again Christians were killed by fanatical Muslims. It must be said that there were also periods of greater tolerance, varying according to ruler or geographical region, but, generally speaking, the notion of Islamic tolerance (often contrasted with Christian intolerance) is a myth. History is far more complex than that, and tolerance within Islam only applied in the literal sense of "sufferance." Consequently, Christians and Jews alike paid a high price, and they remained subject to constant discrimination.

From the thirteenth century onward, the laws governing minorities were interpreted increasingly narrowly. Many were forced to convert to Islam and those who refused were branded, blinded in one eye, castrated, or burned alive.

Despite these threatening developments, the Church of the East continued to flourish in the thirteenth century, particularly with the extension of its mission deep into Asia. Around 1400, however, this dynamic church met a sudden

and violent end at the hands of Muslim Mongols. The army
of the Mongol leader Timur slaughtered not only the two
hundred thousand East Syrian Christians of Baghdad and
Tikrit, but also the West Syrians of Damascus and Mosul,
where Christians were still in the majority. Timur boasted
that he had washed the sword of Islam in the blood of
the infidels. Numerous bishoprics were extinguished and
churches reduced to ashes. Ancient monasteries with priceless manuscripts went up in flames. From then on, what
was left of Syriac Christianity managed to survive only in
inaccessible mountainous regions and a few enclaves such
as Northern Mesopotamia.

In Asia Minor, too, the Syriac churches came increasingly
under threat. The advance of the Turks from the eleventh
century onward took place at the expense of the indigenous Christians and their rich culture, leaving burned-out
monasteries and churches in its wake. The famous library of
Edessa (Urfa) was set on fire and the city's Christian inhabitants murdered or enslaved. The Turks turned out to be
even more aggressively anti-Christian than the Arabs. Were
they, I wonder, subconsciously repeating the pattern of their
own history, given that they too had originally followed a
Shamanic religion until forced by Arabs to choose between
Islam or death? The torture methods practiced by the Turks
on those who refused to convert to Islam were much feared,
and included crucifixion, impaling, and sawing alive. In
the Ottoman Empire, Christians even had to pay human
tributes in the form of the devshirme, or blood tax, whereby
families had to surrender a male child who would then be
raised as a radical Muslim and trained up for the sultan's
elite unit, the janissaries.

Finally, marauding Kurds became the scourge of the
remaining Christians in the countryside and mountains,
forbidden as they were from bearing arms. The Kurds

attacked villages, destroyed the harvest, abducted women and girls, and plundered monasteries, stealing valuable manuscripts and scrolls only to burn them.

Throughout all this, the massacres continued. In 1743, for example, a Persian general ordered the slaughter of some hundred and fifty monks at Mar Elya Monastery near Mosul after they declined the "invitation" to convert to Islam. In 2016 IS completely demolished this fourteen- -hundred-year-old monastery, bulldozing the ruins to preempt any rebuilding.

So a common thread of martyrdom runs through the history of the Syriac churches to the present day like a trail of blood. Followers of the Church of the East have always lived under foreign rule, their status fluctuating precari- ously between recognition, toleration, and persecution; but there has been a trend of growing oppression. As an institu- tion, it has been bled dry: demographically, through Muslim marriage rules; financially, through the imposed poll tax; and literally, through bloody massacres.

Uncle Wadid gives me a nudge. His wife and the two girls are already in the car, waiting for me to tear myself away from the sight of Mar Mattai Monastery and my journey back in time. I look back at the monastery entrance. If stones could speak, what an epic story they would tell: of an early Christian faith that has preserved the language of Jesus to this day; of countless monks who battled with themselves and sought God in the solitude of the rugged cliffs; of bishops and scholars who kept the culture of antiq- uity alive; of the fear and persecution that has persistently dogged this place, claiming innumerable victims; of the refugees who, until recently, camped out on the broad terraces; and of the enchanting hymns in the old monastery church, where three of the last remaining monks sing of their hope of resurrection.

I get into the car and Wadid steps on the gas. The Kurdish checkpoints bring me down to earth with a bump. The scars of war are everywhere – a bombed bridge, shelled houses, a burned-out vehicle. Thoughts and emotions surge around inside me, faster even than Uncle Wadid's car – and with no steering.

Late in the afternoon, Wadid takes me directly to the entrance of the refugee camp to say goodbye to the Little Sisters. I am filled with gratitude for the many conversations and meetings they have arranged for me. And I am aware that I won't be seeing "my sisters" again anytime soon. However many others decide to leave the country, they will stay here, it being part of their mission to go to places where others fear to stay, in order to light a beacon of hope. Those who are forced to remain need to know that God has not abandoned them, and the sisters are a strong testimony to this here at the camp.

The sisters have invited a young couple, Ayad and Salay. The slim, dark-haired Ayad wants me to pass on a letter to his parents in Germany. Ayad and Salay both speak excellent English. They are from Baghdad, and have had to face the fact that there is no longer a place for them as Christians in this country. "My parents have already emigrated," Ayad sighs. "They live near Leipzig."

I am curious. "Where exactly?"

"In Markranstädt."

"That's right near Grünau, where I live – I can visit them!"

Salay has put together a parcel for Ayad's parents,

containing the letter and some homemade candy, which I gladly agree to deliver.

"And what about you?" I ask. "Will you stay in Erbil?"

Salay has found a teaching job, but is owed three months' salary. Ayad gets by doing casual work.

I ask whether they have any children.

Ayad shakes his head. "We don't want to have any in this situation. We can't see any future here. Perhaps we'll be able to emigrate to another country. If there is a future for us there, we'd love to raise a family. But not here."

There is sadness in his voice, and Salay's eyes look tearful. I don't probe any further, but say goodbye to them both, and then to the sisters. We hug each other more tightly than usual, as if giving each other strength.

Thoughtful, sad, and overwhelmed by the many impressions of the day, I walk back to the block where Yousif's family lives. The big black placard is still there on the wall. I think about the monastery with no future, and about Ayad and Salay not daring to have children. Here in Ankawa, where Christianity had thrived since its beginnings, a black placard is staring me in the eye – the death notice of an entire church.

Late that evening, I take my leave of Yousif's family, who have been such warm and welcoming hosts. I have had the opportunity to experience the legendary hospitality of the East firsthand. Yousif, who is staying on for two more days, accompanies me to the Erbil airport along with his brother Basman and Uncle Wadid. There are barriers all around the airport, and we have to go through various checkpoints and gates. Then it's time to say goodbye to my three companions. Not for long in Yousif's case; as for the others, perhaps forever – who knows? My flight is scheduled for 3:55 a.m., Saturday, November 14. Everything goes smoothly. During the stopover in Istanbul, however, I am passing a newsstand when my attention is caught by bold lettering on a Turkish newspaper extra. I can identify two words and a number: Paris – Terror – 100. It's not hard to guess that something dreadful has happened.

On arrival in Berlin, I learn more about the Paris attacks, which have claimed more than 130 lives. Stunned, I can only concur with the reactions – the victims of such violence deserve the attention and sympathy of the whole world. At the same time, my trip to Iraq has made me acutely aware of how many innocent people have died and are dying there with barely a mention. Radical Islamic terrorists are reported to have carried out twelve thousand attacks in Iraq in the last twenty years. Over time, IS has murdered its way through whole swaths of land while Western countries have mostly stood idly by. This double standard is apparent in the French government's response to the Paris attacks – its declared intention to go after IS implies that previous efforts on that front have been half-hearted. Similarly, the vow to drain IS's funding sources goes to show how little has been done to stop the financing of terror so far.

Reflecting on these matters fills me with grief and indignation. Now I can connect them with real people I have grown close to: women, men, and children who have been driven out by the jihadists, and whose relatives have fallen victim to IS murderers. My friends in Erbil and Leipzig stand for thousands who are neither seen nor heard. Again and again, I come up against the puzzling blind spot of Western media as far as the plight of Christians in the

Middle East is concerned. Indeed, as Mosul's Archbishop Casmoussa put it, "The press is silent about our fate, almost as if it were the object of a news blackout." There has been scant coverage of the terror inflicted on Eastern Christians as scapegoats for Western countries, the flight of Christians from Mosul, or the displacement of the Aramaic people from the Nineveh Plain.

Maybe part of the reason is a reluctance by the West to face up to the chaos its policies have created. Not to mention the reluctance to alienate major oil suppliers such as Saudi Arabia or Qatar, particularly since they have invested so extensively in Western economies. "He who pays the piper," or in this case perhaps "he who lays the pipeline."

The relative indifference of our free press to the fate of indigenous Eastern Christians could also be partly due to a lack of awareness. Even as a theologian, I myself have only recently come to discover the richness of the Eastern churches, and at a time when they are severely under threat. Christians in the Middle East have no lobby in Western society, and find little solidarity in our churches. Here again, perhaps ignorance plays a role, or an old aversion on the part of Western churches to those of the East, whose different theological and structural evolution has led them to be regarded as foreign, exotic, or sometimes even heretical.

The lack of understanding sometimes shown by our media on this issue may have other causes too. For one thing, it is hard for us to imagine how radically the political environment inhabited by Eastern Christians differs from our own, to the extent that they can be made to suffer as hostages for the freedoms of the West. This was brought home to me by the uproar in the Middle East over European political cartoons depicting Mohammed. Such cartoons are a normal phenomenon in free democratic societies but, thanks to our globalized world, can trigger violent reactions in other, undemocratic systems. Thus, when caricatures of Mohammed were published in Denmark in 2006, the terrorist Mujahideen Council announced that Christians in Iraq would pay the price – which they duly did.

This connection was insufficiently grasped by the media. When the authors of the Muhammad cartoons were killed in Paris, statesmen from all over the world sent condolences and, a year on, memorial plaques were unveiled to commemorate the anniversary of the attack. Yet when people in the Middle East are murdered who know nothing of the cartoons, and bear no responsibility for them, their fate appears to warrant neither a press report nor a plaque. There is a clear discrepancy here. In my view, we should endeavor to consider *all* victims of terrorism, and especially those who are innocent and have no lobby or vote.

One final point concerns me regarding the persecution of Christians in Muslim countries, one that probably goes against the grain of political correctness – there is worry that reports of these atrocities could be hijacked by anti-Islamic right-wing movements for propaganda purposes. Attempts to draw attention to the persecution are often countered with a knee-jerk reference to the Crusades – as if the current persecution of Christians should be declared a taboo subject because of the wrongs inflicted on Muslims by Christians in the past.

It may be that a guilt complex on the part of Western Christians is at work here, given that the use of armed force in the name of Christianity contradicts the letter of the gospel and the spirit of Jesus. In this context, Pope John Paul II was right to make a public confession of guilt and express regret for the injustice of the Crusades. But self-criticism should not make us afraid to draw attention to problems on the other side.

We cannot progress toward greater justice and reconciliation until we are open about the glaring injustice that Christians have suffered and continue to suffer in Islamic countries. It is important to differentiate here between the vast numbers of Muslims who live peaceably, and members of fundamentalist groups who claim to act in the name of Islam. We should also not forget that jihadism springs from a variety of social and political motives as well as religious ones. Ultimately, however, the role of religion is undeniable.

12

A Rocket in the Roof

After returning from Iraq, I am soon back into my old
routine, working twice as fast to catch up with the tasks I
had left behind. But inwardly I remain preoccupied with
Kurdistan. In my free time, I begin to devote myself more
intensively to the local Christian refugees, whose fate is now
constantly on my mind.

My first visit takes me to Markranstädt, where I have
promised to deliver the letter and parcel from Ankawa.
After a brief search, I find myself at the door of a small
apartment.

Ayad's mother, Warda, is a plumpish woman of around
sixty-five with very good English. His father, Ghasan, who
looks a few years older, speaks English too, though with
a slight stutter. His tall figure and white hair give him a
dignified appearance. The old couple are delighted to hear
from their son and daughter-in-law in Kurdistan, and invite
me to join them for tea and the snacks I had brought from
Ankawa.

Ghasan and Warda are both from Baghdad, which until
recently was home to a sizeable Christian minority. They
met and fell in love at Baghdad University, where they were
both studying physics. After graduating, they married and
had three children. Then the murderous conflict between
Iraq and Iran intervened, lasting from 1980 to 1988. Ghasan

was called up and sent to the front, where he experienced the full horror of war. He recalls how, after the Iraqis had entrenched themselves behind a minefield, the Iranians sent hundreds of children over the mines to make them explode and so clear a path for the soldiers. The children wore a green band around their heads with the Muslim creed, and a plastic key around their necks, signifying that they would go straight to paradise after their death.

Ghasan's face freezes, and I can see the anguish in his features. "I saw the children on the Iranian side running off into the field, and then the explosions – an inferno of blood and human limbs."

I stare at the floor, appalled by Ghasan's descriptions. No doubt these images will remain imprinted in his memory forever.

For decades, Iraq was relatively secular in its politics. Warda tells me relations with their Muslim neighbors had been good. But with the re-Islamization of the entire Muslim world came a growing emphasis on religious affiliation, resulting in an increasing tendency to label non-Muslims as unbelievers, outsiders, and enemies. The return to a fundamentalist form of Islam destroyed the natural solidarity of everyday community life.

Ghasan and Warda, too, were made to feel the stigma of being Christian. At work, people would say to Ghasan, "You're a good colleague and a nice person. There's just one problem: you must become a Muslim!" Such remarks were motivated by genuine concern, the prevailing belief being that Christians were godless and would go to hell. Schoolchildren were similarly affected by the gradual loss of tolerance that came with increasing Islamic religiosity. Ghasan and Warda's two girls were always being told by their teachers, "You're such pretty girls. But to be pure you must become Muslims."

While isolated attacks and assaults on Baghdad's Christians had already begun in the nineties, the situation remained bearable on the whole. All of that changed with the invasion of American troops in 2003. In the Iraq War, civilians killed by bombs or rockets were referred to as "collateral damage," a cynical term glossing over the tacit acceptance of innocent deaths. Muslims and Christians alike fell victim to American air strikes.

Warda relates the following story: "In the middle of the night, we were woken by a loud bang. We didn't know what it was, and thought maybe a bomb had landed in front of the house. I got up and turned the light on. When I opened the bedroom door, I was hit by a cloud of dust. Ghasan came out onto the stairs, coughing. Then we saw the incredible thing that had happened: a rocket had struck our house and bored through the roof without exploding. The tip of it had gone through into the living room, where we had a small statue of the Virgin Mary."

Ghasan adds in a quiet, almost reverential tone, "Yes, it was a miracle. We could have been killed on the spot, along with all the neighbors."

During the course of our conversation, I learn more about the background to the war, which led to terrible acts of violence against Christians – another instance of collateral damage. It should have been clear from the history of the Crusades or the First World War that local Christians would suffer because of the American invasion. How could the United States and Britain be so indifferent to the bloodshed of innocent Christian minorities caused by their oil-driven politics?

The number of murdered Christians rose from fifteen in 2003 to one hundred thirteen in 2004. In the same year,

Islamists carried out nineteen attacks in a coordinated campaign against Christians and their institutions in Baghdad. Often well educated and wealthy, Christians were prime targets for abduction in order to extort hefty ransoms.

The jihadists' acts of violence grew increasingly brutal. Some Christians were hurled, bound and blindfolded, from the terraces of high-rise buildings. Others had their throats slit with a knife like slaughtered lambs. Yet others were hanged or crucified. Women were raped, and even babies weren't spared the religious fighters' murderous hatred of "unbelievers."

Some of the reports that flew around the internet in those days were too awful to believe and impossible to verify, but nonetheless had a chilling effect. In one, a fourteen-year-old boy was crucified; as he hung from the cross, the jihadists slashed his belly open with a sword, leaving him to die an agonizing death in the sight of his own spilled guts. In another, a toddler was kidnapped and, when the Christian mother failed to raise the ransom, the child was beheaded, burned, and sent back to her on a platter with rice.

More and more churches were obliterated by bombs. Priests were targeted and anyone attending a church service ran the risk of abduction or attack.

Warda recalls with horror how, on May 17, 2007, the imam Hatim al-Razzaq issued local Christians an ultimatum to convert to Islam within twenty-four hours or leave the country. To reinforce the fatwa, Muslim clerics sent out messages over the loudspeakers of the mosques inciting their followers to plunder Christian property. This threat resulted in a wholesale exodus of Christians from Baghdad and the surrounding area. For those who stayed behind, life became increasingly unendurable.

"Did you never hear about the attack on Our Lady of
Salvation Church in Baghdad?" Warda asks. I don't recall
the incident and ask to hear the story.

It is October 31, 2010. Ghasan and Warda are at home while
their eldest daughter, Farah, who is six months pregnant,
attends evening prayer at the local Syriac Catholic church.
During the service, seven radical Islamic fighters storm the
church with guns, hand grenades, and explosive belts.

Halting his prayer, one of the two priests asks, "What
do you want?" He is answered with a cry of "Allahu akbar!"
and a volley of shots from the assailants' Kalashnikovs blast
the twenty-seven-year-old minister to the ground. The next
bullets are aimed at the cross above the altar. A devastating
bloodbath follows, in which men, women, and children are
shot indiscriminately. First, however, the religious fighters
barricade themselves in with the three hundred–strong
congregation, using them as hostages in a bid to obtain the
release of Islamic fundamentalists in Iraq and Egypt.

Warda interrupts her story, breaking into loud sobs. "You
don't have to go on," I whisper.

But Ghasan, also in tears, picks up the thread, his stutter
steadily worsening: "After about two hours, the terrorists
started killing hostages and firing at random. Our daughter
Farah was in terror of her life and kept thinking of the baby
in her womb. The man directly next to her was hit and fell
sideways with his head in her lap. The blood gushed out all
over her dress, and she leaned her head back against the
wall and closed her eyes so that she looked dead. That saved
her life."

Through her half-closed eyes, however, she watched her
uncle, who had been playing the organ during the service,
fall to the ground, struck dead by a bullet. In the general

chaos a baby, clutched tightly by an anxious mother, began to cry. At this, one of the terrorists shouted "Quiet!" and shot both mother and child. Then came the most despicable spectacle of all, as one of the religious fanatics seized a four-year-old child and cut off its head on the altar, before throwing down the cross and trampling it underfoot.

Soon after, a special unit of the Iraqi army stormed the church, whereupon the jihadists detonated two explosive belts. The grim toll of this attack on a peaceful congregation amounted to fifty-eight dead and sixty-seven injured. The organization Islamic State of Iraq claimed responsibility for the terrorist act and said in a statement that "all Christians and their organizations, institutions, and leaders are legitimate targets of the religious fighters."

Still, this elderly couple steadfastly resisted all these attempts to drive them from their home. In 2013, they tell me, a further thirty or more Christians were killed by a bomb attack during a Christmas service.

The following year, there was a ring at the door. Ghasan opened it to find three masked men, all armed with Kalashnikovs.

The terrorists' demands were clear: "You are an unbeliever. You must leave this house."

Ghasan refused to be intimidated: "What gives you the right to evict me?"

One of the three men cried, "You are Christians!"

Ghasan wouldn't give up. "This is our country too. We were here before you. And we have never asked you to leave. Why should *we* be the ones to go?"

The leader of the jihadists chose to answer this bold question with violence rather than arguments, and fired a bullet at the couple's white miniature poodle, which had

come running to bark at the intruders. As the dog fell dead
to the floor, the terrorist turned to them with a contemp-
tuous grin. "You have three days. Any more questions?"

With that, he and his accomplices turned and
disappeared.

Warda shows me a photo of the cute little dog on her
phone, followed by another with a red blood stain on its
fluffy white fur.

Since that day, Ghasan, who had once been a university
lecturer, has had a speech impediment. And the more he
talks about the attacks, the worse his stutter becomes.

Warda and Ghasan had no time to think after this last
incident; they packed a few personal items and managed,
by a lucky chance, to obtain a visa for Italy. From there they
drove to Germany, their daughter Farah and her family
having already moved to Hamburg four years earlier. By
rights, they should have stayed in Italy under the EU's
Dublin II regulation, but they didn't know anybody there.
They applied to settle in Germany but were turned down by
the courts. (I ask them to show me the ruling, and find the
ten-page document full of references to laws and other court
rulings baffling, both linguistically and from a humanitarian
viewpoint.) Consequently, Warda and Ghasan's only chance
of being able to stay with their daughter's family was to lay
low for the next six months to avoid being deported to Italy,
and then apply for asylum in Germany. Now they live in
constant dread of the police turning up on their doorstep in
the middle of the night to deport them. After all they have
been through, they are once again forced to hide, this time
in fear of the German police.

Added to this is the gnawing anxiety about their son
and daughter-in-law in Ankawa. "There is no future for
them as Christians in a Muslim country," Ghasan says

pessimistically. "What kind of religion incites its followers to violence, or at least does nothing to prevent it?"

I attempt to balance this remark with other points of view. Ghasan nods wearily. "Yes, there are educated Muslims who are a model of humanity. But the religious fighters who take the Koran literally are barbaric."

He tells me about a discussion he had with some Salafists who were distributing copies of the Koran in Leipzig's pedestrian zone. They were young Germans who spoke fairly good Arabic. I take out my notebook and jot down the old man's account.

Ghasan addressed one of the bearded men who had offered him the Koran: "You are my brother because you are a human being. But if you follow this book to the letter you will become a terrorist, like the followers of IS."

"We have nothing to do with IS," the Muslim defended himself. "Where are you from?"

"From Iraq. See how white my hair is. I have spent my whole life in the company of Muslims. There are good Muslims. But if they take this book literally . . ."

"Muhammad brings peace," the Muslim missionary objected.

Ghasan shook his head. "You are anything but peaceful."

"Our religion is peace."

"No," Ghasan persisted. "You live by the sword. I know what I'm talking about. Believe me, I've been there."

Ghasan and I get into a long discussion about the relationship between religion and violence in Islam. Two things strike us as important. Firstly, the question of exegesis. Opinions are divided on this point. Is it possible, for example, to interpret the Koran on the basis of the early revelations while relativizing the later warlike verses as a product of their time? Or do such relativizations cast doubt on the Koran's absolute authority as the literal Word of God?

The second point relates to the character of the Prophet Muhammad, which can also be seen from different perspectives. In the beginning, he appears as a peaceful messenger; later on, as the leader of belligerent tribes. What is clear is that the fusion of religious and political power dates back to the very beginning of Islam.

Historically, there is no denying the existence of Islamic states that have shown a limited yet significant tolerance toward minorities. But such societies have never granted non-Muslims true freedom of religion, making them equal before the law. Ghasan cites a current example from Iraq, where the (US-supported) government passed a law in 2015 stating that, if a Christian converts to Islam, their entire family automatically becomes Muslim, including adult children. Thereafter, the rule "once a Muslim, always a Muslim" applies. There is no right to return to Christianity. The evidence indicates that wherever Islam is in a position of power, adherents of other religions have been discriminated against by state laws.

In the case of Christianity, the relationship between state and religion is of a different nature. Jesus himself strictly rejected the imposition of his religious message through state authority: "My kingdom is not of this world" (John 18:36). His distinction "Give back to Caesar what is Caesar's – and to God what is God's" (Matt. 22:21) was revolutionary in the history of religion, as it laid the foundation for the separation of state and religion. The Eastern churches held to this: at no time in their long history have they wielded state power.

In the Western churches, things developed differently. After the persistent persecution of Christians by the Roman state, Emperor Constantine turned the tables in the year

AD 313. The recognition of Christianity by the state reset
its relationship with the Roman Empire. For the first three
centuries, Christians had refused to perform military
service; now it became a Christian duty to obey the state
and defend it by force of arms. The violence of medieval
Christianity has its roots in this close interconnection
of state and religion. The devastating confessional wars
between Catholics and Protestants forced a reevaluation of
this issue, giving rise to the model of the secular state, in
which civic rights and duties were no longer dependent on
religious affiliation. This separation of church and state was
also inspired by the teachings of Jesus and the practice of
the early church.

Ghasan doubts that Islam is capable of distinguishing
between state and religion, as this would require a radical
modernization of the faith. If the Koran is no longer
understood as the eternally valid Word of God, he argues,
Islam loses its whole foundation. This is precisely what the
fundamentalists are afraid of, which is why they fight so
vehemently against any relativization of the Koran and any
criticism of the Prophet Muhammad.

Our fascinating debate is abruptly interrupted by the
doorbell. Ghasan starts in alarm, so deep-seated is his fear
of the police. He waits a few seconds before rising to his
feet. Arabic voices penetrate into the living room through
the open door. Shortly after, a tall, slim man and a boy
enter the room. "Marhaba," I greet them. The stranger is
unshaven and looks at me curiously through thick, horn-
rimmed glasses. The boy translates his father's Arabic
greeting. It's an arrangement familiar to me by now: children interpreting for their parents.

Ghasan introduces his guests: "This is Garo and his son Agob. They are from Syria and live around the corner."

I learn that Garo has another son, and I agree to arrange some homework coaching for them both. Before I know it, I have another date in my diary.

13

Garo's Odyssey

A few days later, I visit Garo's family. In their living room,
a Syrian TV channel is playing and I am plunged into
the thick of war, my eyes drawn to the screaming rocket
launchers and rumbling tanks. Garo turns the sound off,
but the images remain.

Garo's wife, Zuvinar, appears – a petite woman with long,
black hair. She greets me with a fleeting smile, but looks
worried. I arrange the first homework coaching sessions
for the two boys, Agob and Awanis. Agob, who looks about
twelve, translates our conversation.

I kick things off by asking, "You're from Syria –
whereabouts?"

The family is from Hassake, a town in northeast Syria,
and has been living for around six months in a prefab block,
a relic of the old communist days. The apartment is taste-
fully decorated with second-hand furniture, and the walls
are adorned with icons. I notice a photo of a man in a black,
turban-like cap.

"That's our bishop," Garo explains, "a bishop of the
Armenian Church."

"So you're Armenians?" I ask.

Garo tells me his grandfather was deported as a young
boy from his original home of Mardin, Anatolia, in 1915.
Most of the family died in the massacres and death

marches, but his grandfather was rescued from starvation and subsequently settled in Hassake.

Garo, a qualified optician, had built up a small business in Hassake. Fifteen years ago, he and Zuvinar married and the couple spent a few happy years with their two children.

That, says Garo, was before the so-called Arab Spring triggered the rapid collapse of the Syrian state, with twenty-eight different groups fighting the Assad regime and attempting to take control of people and territory. Islamist troops, recruited from fanatical young men – and women – around the world, became heavily involved in the war. These radical Muslims swiftly gained influence, and the Islamic State in Iraq and Syria (ISIS) was soon declared.

A hundred years after the murder and expulsion of his ancestors, Garo and his family are threatened with the same fate in Hassake. Racked with fear, they follow the news stories of Muslim fundamentalists attacking Christian villages, extorting protection money, murdering men, abducting women and children, and burning down churches. Jihadists from Germany, Britain, and France are particularly barbaric in their treatment of the local Christians.

Garo and Zuvinar hope that things will remain calm in Hassake. But then the worst happens: Garo is driving to another village to visit a friend when three motorcyclists suddenly appear behind him and force him to stop. Black masks conceal their faces. One of them flings open the door and drags Garo out of the car. He doesn't resist, knowing he doesn't stand a chance. Bound, gagged, and blindfolded, he is driven away in his own vehicle. They are on the road for about an hour before Garo is yanked out again and feels fists pushing him in a certain direction. He staggers forward and hears his kidnappers being congratulated on their haul.

Soon after, he is led into a room. His captors leave him; the door clicks shut behind them and is locked. Garo sits on the floor with his back to the wall and waits. After endless minutes, the door opens and a gruff voice demands his wife's telephone number.

Garo dictates the number. The phone rings and Zuvinar answers. Garo is forced to repeat the words: "If you want to see me again alive, you must pay five million lira."

Garo hears Zuvinar cry out and start to sob. It nearly breaks his heart.

He is then given further lines to repeat: "You have one day. Tomorrow I will call again and tell you where to bring the money."

By now, Garo is sweating blood. He tries to negotiate with his captor, explaining that Zuvinar would never be able to get this sum together. Even if she borrowed money from friends and neighbors, it still wouldn't be enough.

He spends a sleepless night in his cell, knowing only too well that for years terrorists belonging to Al-Qaeda, IS, and other groupings of Islamic religious fighters have been kidnapping and holding Christians for ransom. What's more, he knows that many of those abducted are not released even when large sums are paid out, but simply killed. All night he is tortured by thoughts of his wife, the children, and his sick mother; if she finds out about this, the shock might kill her.

But Zuvinar has said nothing either to the children or Garo's mother. She tells the children that their father has arrived safely at his friend's and is staying there for a few days to help him with a job. Then she runs to a trusted neighbor, who helps her borrow money from friends and relatives. Even the minister of the Armenian community contributes something. But the total still doesn't add up to five million lira.

The next day, Garo is made to telephone again. Zuvinar is in tears, having only managed to raise two million. Garo hears the gruff-voiced man order her to bring two and a half million lira the next evening to a solitary tree on the outskirts of the city which can be seen from such-and-such a street. She is to come alone.

Zuvinar manages to scrape together the outstanding sum, and goes on foot to the edge of the city carrying a plain plastic bag with the money. She finds the tree and walks toward it, her heart pounding as she thinks of Garo and their two children. She places the bag discreetly on the ground. There isn't a soul in sight, but she senses that she is being closely watched.

She turns and walks away from the tree, numb with fear and walking faster with every step. She arrives home soaked in sweat, but prepares the evening meal as usual and tries to hide her desperate anxiety from the children. That night, sleepless with worry, she gets up continually and opens the front door, listening vainly for sounds. At last, a cockcrow heralds the break of dawn. She makes breakfast, wakes the children, and sends them to school. Around midday, she finally hears a familiar step – Garo!

Her husband was lucky. His kidnappers accepted a lesser sum than originally demanded and kept their promise to release him on payment of the ransom. The masked men's last words to Garo as they ejected him from his own car – since commandeered by the terrorists – were, "Now beat it! You have no right to be here!"

The message couldn't be clearer. Garo sells their apartment for a song and pawns the family's remaining belongings. As his brother has been living near Cologne for the last year, Germany seems the obvious place of refuge.

Garo manages to negotiate his way with his family through the war zone to Damascus, taking with him all the money he could muster from the sale of their home and valuables. After finally reaching Damascus, he asks an Armenian family how best to get to Europe. Following a hot tip, he makes contact with a people-smuggling gang.

Garo feels guilty and, above all, afraid. As he hands over all his cash to the smuggler, he is painfully aware that he is placing his life and that of his family at the mercy of a criminal gang. Many people have been robbed by human traffickers, without ever reaching the promised destination. Luckily for him, however, the gang he has found in Damascus turns out to be bona fide, although the secret route they have devised seems nothing short of absurd.

Agob says the things he and his family have been through are beyond belief. I invite him to elaborate. Every now and then, I ask Garo and Zuvinar questions and Agob translates back and forth, with Awanis adding some of his own recollections.

From Damascus, the four head for the Turkish border, taking a highly circuitous route to avoid live combat zones and road blockades. After a two-day bus journey they reach Istanbul, from where they expect to be shipped across to Greece or Italy. They call the cell phone number they have been given and arrange to meet a contact named by the smugglers. He takes away their Syrian passports and returns them a few days later with a visa for – of all places – Tanzania. Garo and Zuvinar board the plane with a great deal of skepticism, although Agob and Awanis are excited at the prospect of going to Africa. All the smugglers have given them is a number to call in Dar es Salaam.

On arrival, they have to surrender their passports once again. This time, there is a long wait. Every phone inquiry meets with the same response: be patient. But what should they live on in the meantime? They are hungry, especially the children; Agob is just ten, and Awanis eight. They all look for work in the market. The children find a job weighing and bagging sugar from a big sack, and Garo and Zuvinar labor, like the children, in exchange for meals. They sleep in a bus shelter. With no possessions but the clothes on their backs, at least they have nothing to fear from robbers. Awanis's face lights up as he remembers earning the occasional chewing gum on top of his basic food allowance.

While in Tanzania, Zuvinar has a dream. She sees a divinely beautiful man standing before a door and recognizes him immediately from his radiant aura as Jesus. The door behind him is ajar, and he speaks to her: "Be patient!"

Garo's family continue living in Tanzania for five months until one of the smugglers finally turns up with their passports and a set of air tickets to Brazil. Now Garo is thoroughly bewildered, until the man eventually explains that from Brazil it is relatively easy to enter Portugal.

After a month-long stay in Rio de Janeiro, they are given air tickets to Lisbon and the phone number of a contact in Portugal. He takes their passports away yet again, promising to get back in touch. But they never hear from him again, nor do they get their passports back. They call the number repeatedly, but to no avail.

At last they are in Europe – but what next? They travel on foot, scrape a bit of money together by begging and manage to catch a bus to the Spanish border, where they are waved through unchallenged. In Madrid, they traipse around to churches, asking for help, but no one understands them. Close to one of the churches, they find a mosque where Arabic is spoken and are able to explain their predicament. They are allowed to sleep in the mosque, and are given food, clothing, and even a bit of money for their onward journey.

At the French border, a miraculous thing happens. They are standing – without passports – in the queue. Just as Garo reaches the control desk, a tussle breaks out between a customs officer and some people in another queue, and the official about to scrutinize Garo rushes off to help his colleague. "Quick!" Garo whispers, and the four cross the border into France unchecked. Zuvinar is convinced that God helped them through.

By now it's February 2015, and bitterly cold. There is snow on the ground. They sleep mostly in bus shelters; Zuvinar, Agob, and Awanis use the clothes they were given in Spain as makeshift blankets, while Garo sits on the bench all night watching over the fragile lives of his loved ones.

The last two border crossings – from France via Belgium to Germany – are likewise problem-free. Zuvinar remembers standing outside a store in Cologne, utterly exhausted, frozen, and desperate. She felt so helpless in this alien country, she tells me, where both the spoken and written language were a mystery to her, and where she had met with such a cold reception. She was huddled by the roadside, sobbing loudly, when a man stopped and spoke to her. Seeing that none of the family understood German or English, he took them to the main train station and notified the railroad police, then pressed a twenty-euro bill into her hand. At the end of Zuvinar's account, Awanis, who has been listening attentively and adding bits here and there, declares, "I'll never forget any of that. It will stay in my mind forever."

After their arrival in Germany, the family had another difficult route to negotiate – this time through the registration and asylum application procedure. First they were packed off to Dortmund, then to Chemnitz. There, they applied for asylum and had to live in the asylum seeker hostel for seven months. Agob has bad memories of this time. "After Syria, it was like being at war all over again."

At the hostel there were major tensions between Algerians, Tunisians, and Chechens. One might have thought that a Christian family would be unaffected by this inter-Muslim conflict, but once again – as in the Syrian civil war – they found themselves caught in the crossfire. They were plagued by anxiety: Would the warring Muslims take out their hatred on them, or worse still, on their children?

The moment they arrived, Zuvinar says, Muslim residents spat at her because of the small cross she wore around her neck. Garo and the children were insulted as "unbelievers." Nor were they allowed to use the communal kitchen for fear they would render it "impure." As the violence in the hostel began to escalate, the four of them no longer dared go outside, and shut themselves in their room for days on end. Garo was beset with doubts: Had they made the wrong decision in fleeing their home? Had they opted for the wrong country? Now his family faced the threat of yet more violence. There were pools of blood in the corridor and smeared on the walls, recalling the horrifying scenes they had witnessed in Hassake.

Agob and Awanis were the only Christian children in the hostel. One day, some Muslim boys saw Agob with a bag of gummy bears in his hand – an act of treachery in their eyes, as the sweets contain pork gelatin and are therefore not halal according to Muslim dietary rules which distinguish between "clean" and "unclean" foods.

The Muslim children shouted abuse at Agob, spitting at him and crying in chorus, "You eat pork!" and, "You're dirty!" Before he knew it, he was set upon and beaten by the mob.

I can still hear the hurt in Agob's voice at the unfairness of a world that excludes and vilifies people for being Christian. He simply can't understand why eating gummy bears should make him a bad person.

Three days after this incident, Agob fell into his tormentors' hands again and received another beating in an attempt to make him convert to Islam. "You're an unbeliever! You'll go to hell!" Agob stuck it out and endured the blows stoically. Giving up his Christian faith and becoming a Muslim simply wasn't an option for the eleven-year-old. "I would rather have died!"

Such loyalty to Christ commands my utmost respect. I never fail to be impressed by the deep faith displayed by Eastern Christians. For the sake of Jesus Christ, they have suffered all kinds of harassment and even given up their homeland. Friends and relatives – including children – have paid for their Christian beliefs with their lives. In Mosul, IS terrorists stopped a boy in the street because he was wearing a small cross around his neck. They ordered him to throw it away, and when he steadfastly refused, they buried him alive. Whenever I hear stories like this and meet Christians of such courage, I can't help but wonder: How much is my faith worth to me? How high a price would I be prepared to pay?

When I drop in to see the Armenian family a few days later, the living room is once again filled with the clamor of war. Garo is staring at the TV screen in despair. With Agob's help, I learn that he and Zuvinar had to make a painful decision back in Hassake: Garo knew that the journey would be too much for his eighty-four-year-old mother, but it was also clear since his abduction that he could no longer stay. He had to put his children and their safety first. Only a few

days before, terrorists had beheaded a good friend and his
son in a nearby Christian village. Zuvinar and Garo were
distraught. What should they do? Save the children and
leave Garo's mother behind with her unmarried daughter
to look after her? Or stay with his mother and risk their
own lives, and above all those of their children? Eventually,
Zuvinar and Garo had decided to flee for the children's sake.

But the thought of the elderly mother and sister they
have left behind is now torturing them. Zuvinar bursts into
tears. "Andreas, help us!" Garo implores.

I have no idea what to do, so I make a few inquiries.
Apparently, first-degree relatives can be brought over,
subject to a declaration of commitment. Perhaps I could
ask friends to take on the maintenance and health insur-
ance costs for Garo's mother and sister. The German state
allows family members to enter the country provided no
costs are incurred by the public purse. But then I learn
that this regulation only applies to relatives of migrants
who entered the country before December 31, 2012. Garo's
family arrived after that, so they are out of luck on that
score. I consult a range of authorities and advice centers,
but there appears to be no legal means of bringing Garo's
mother and sister to Germany.

It pains me to have to break the bad news: "I'm afraid it's
not possible for your mother to come to Germany." Garo's
face darkens and he stares into the distance. I can guess
what's going through his mind – the guilt he feels for having
left a sick, elderly parent behind in Hassake. But what else
could he have done? War compels people to make agonizing
decisions. How can anyone who is forced to abandon his
mother in order to save his children ever sleep peacefully
again? I am becoming increasingly aware of the immorality
of any war that forces people to betray the natural dictates
of their conscience. On the way home, I wonder what I

would have done if faced with the inhumane choice of
taking care of my mother or saving my children.

A few weeks later, Zuvinar and Garo hear another
mention of the possibility of Germany taking in Syrian refugees and, clutching at any straw, they call me again. Once
again, I have to disappoint them bitterly – there is no hope
for Garo's mother and sister. Should I counsel them to pray?
Yes, why not? We can always lay our troubles before God.
When we are in distress and don't know where to turn, we
can at least express our helplessness in prayer. We can offer
up the difficult and scarcely bearable things to God in the
hope that he will give us strength to carry our burdens.
When I promise Zuvinar and Garo to pray for their relatives, it's not just an empty phrase; I try to empathize with
their pain. I join them in gazing at the cross on the living
room wall. Perhaps it is by keeping the image of the cross
before their eyes that Christians in the East manage not to
become embittered by their despair. Their suffering hasn't
led them to inflict suffering on others in retaliation. By
praying, they have followed Jesus' example of placing their
problems in God's hands, in the belief that he can turn even
the deepest darkness into light.

A few days later I hear on the news that IS has captured
parts of Hassake. I go straight over to Zuvinar and Garo.
The TV is on a Syrian channel. The children stare, mesmerized, at the screen, where soldiers' guns are blazing amid
exploding grenades and burning houses. A short while ago,
Garo managed to phone his sister, who told him that she
and his mother had fled to Qamishli. Now IS forces are
advancing there too. Garo tells me he could hear gunfire in
the background even as they spoke. He and Zuvinar are out
of their minds with worry. I wish I could do something to
help – but what?

"I can sell one of my kidneys and use the money to get my mother out of there," Garo suggests.

I shake my head. "There's no legal way for your sister and your mother to migrate to Germany."

I realize that, in Syria, even legal hurdles can sometimes be overcome with money, and try to explain that, however terrible the current situation, nothing can be achieved here by bribery. That, I point out, is one of the great advantages of a democratic country.

On the screen, smoke is rising from a district of the city.

"Why don't you switch the TV off?" I tell Garo. "It's not good for your children to be looking at images of war all the time. *This* is your home now."

"Syria is my home," Awanis contradicts me. "That's where I was born. That's where I learned my language."

I say no more, seeing that my well-meant advice isn't going to cut any ice with the family, who are still far too bound up with the war in Syria. Indeed, the children's grandma and aunt have just fled to the very city from which black smoke clouds are now rising.

14

Remembrance Is
the Secret of Redemption

I am at Garo and Zuvinar's again, helping them to fill in
school forms. Over supper, I ask the couple how they first
met.

It was on a pilgrimage, they tell me – a lovely story.
Zuvinar, it seems, is not originally from Hassake, but Deir
ez-Zor. In 1991, a memorial church was consecrated in her
home city, and it was at this Armenian Church celebration
that Garo and Zuvinar met and fell in love.

The story of their Armenian family, by contrast, is
anything but lovely. Until 1915, Zuvinar's ancestors lived in
Anatolia, in the village of Tell-Ermen (meaning "Armenian
hill"). During the Armenian pogroms, the Turks nailed her
grandfather to a door by the ears and tortured him to death.
As Agob translates this appalling story for me, I feel sick
to the core. Back home, I do some more research into Deir
ez-Zor and the persecution of the Armenians.

What follows was hard to write, and may be almost
unbearable to read. But I think it has to be faced, because
the terrible events of 1915 are repeating themselves in many
respects today, a hundred years on.

Like the Aramaic Christians, the Armenians lived for
centuries under Muslim rule as a "protected people," sometimes recognized, sometimes bullied and persecuted. At
regular intervals, Turks and Kurds invaded their homes and
churches, looted their property, and violated Armenian girls.

In the nineteenth century, the mood of nationalism
caught on among the Armenians, and the desire for more
rights and independence was asserted. At that time, European powers were also stepping up the pressure on the
Ottoman Empire to modernize and grant more civil rights
to ethnic and religious minorities. The so-called Young
Turk movement initially took up the cause of reform, but
later fell prey to an extreme nationalist ideology which
sought to eradicate all non-Turkish elements. The Armenians in particular, as the largest Christian minority in Asia
Minor, were a thorn in the Turkish nationalists' side. Armenians placed a high value on education and were therefore
disproportionately represented in academic occupations,
while their strong influence on business and trade aroused
jealousy and resentment. The outbreak of the First World
War provided a pretext to crack down on them. As an ally
of Germany and Austria-Hungary, the Ottoman Empire
was already engaged in a war in the Caucasus against the
common enemy, Russia. This served as an official reason for
eliminating the Christian Armenians as potential collaborators of "Christian" Russia. Above all, however, the First
World War created an ideal smokescreen for resolving
the Armenian question once and for all. By the end of the
resulting ethnic and religious purges, the whole of Anatolia,
which had been deeply Christian since the first century, had
undergone a rapid and complete Islamization. Over two
thousand churches and monasteries had been destroyed,
and their rich legacy of art and literature irrecoverably lost.

There are numerous historic documents testifying to the Turks' systematic preparation and execution of the "final solution" envisaged for the Armenian people. On April 24, 1915, the Armenian intellectual, economic, and clerical elite of Istanbul, where Christians still accounted for nearly half the population, were arrested and the majority subsequently exterminated. This robbed the unarmed Armenians of their leadership overnight, leaving them helplessly exposed to ruthless persecution and destruction.

The whole enterprise, which was officially disguised as a "resettlement," was carried out by troops drawn largely from the ranks of dangerous criminals. The sadism of the Turkish and Kurdish militias knew no bounds. In the churches, priests were nailed to the cross and girls dragged over the altar and raped. Bishops were burned at the stake. One deacon arrested during a service had the hot coals from the incense burner stuffed into his mouth. In Diyarbakir – a city with a Christian population of around 40 percent – hordes of men attacked and raped Christian women. The menfolk had horseshoes nailed to the soles of their bare feet (red hot ones in the case of the bishop). Mutilation of bodies was routine. Genitals were hacked off and stuffed into the corpses' mouths, and in the case of pregnant women, the soldiers would bet on the sex of the unborn child and slit open the dead woman's belly to see who had won.

Prior to deportation or murder, all victims were given the option of converting to Islam. Those who did so were left unharmed. Those who refused paid with their lives. In the case of priests, first their hands, then their feet, and finally their head would be chopped off. One Muslim cleric slit the throats of a whole group of young Armenians one by one while reciting verses from the Koran, mirroring the ritual slaughter of sheep at the sacrificial feast of Eid.

Hundreds of thousands of women and children were forcibly converted to Islam. Girls above the age of thirteen were made to marry Muslims; boys up to thirteen were circumcised and placed in Muslim families, while older ones were deemed no longer capable of assimilation and duly killed. In Ankara, the sultan's birthday was celebrated with the circumcision of a hundred Armenian boys.

On the death marches into the Mesopotamian desert, a large proportion of the deportees perished from hunger and thirst, exhaustion and epidemics, or as a result of mass murder. The lacerated corpses were left to rot by the roadside, poisoning the air with a foul stench. Around 870,000, less than half the total, reached Mesopotamia. With yellow, emaciated faces, they were interned in "concentration camps" (a term which the Turks borrowed from the British, who had established similar camps in the Boer War). By fall 1916, some 630,000 deportees had died in these camps. Death squads drove the survivors into the desert, where they were made to dig their own graves and climb in before being shot one by one. Others were herded into oil-rich caves near the village of Shaddadeh and burned alive. This underground maze of caves is known to this day as Chabs-el-Ermen ("Ditch of the Armenians"). One Jewish officer in the Ottoman army reported that the death cries of the burning victims could be heard for miles around. Yet others were imprisoned in caves and suffocated by lighting fires at the entrance. In Deir ez-Zor, the militias built a huge bonfire onto which they threw two thousand bound Armenian children and burned them with gasoline. These methods of destruction foreshadowed the gas chambers and crematoria of the Third Reich in all their savage brutality.

In 1917, German soldiers discovered huge mounds of bones and skulls in Deir ez-Zor, and the medical officer Armin Wegner photographed numerous sites of atrocities.

Already in July 1915, the German Vice-Consul in Samsun had described the events as "nothing less than the destruction or enforced Islamization of a whole people."

There is a wealth of documents by German diplomats and officers attesting to the atrocities of 1915 and 1916. What shocked them most was the sadistic violence committed in public view and with public support. People were sawn up alive, suspended from butcher's hooks, impaled, crucified, skinned, or buried alive; girls' breasts were cut off and boys castrated, small children hacked to pieces and babies' fingers chopped off.

The German Empire also had a hand in this first major systematic genocide of the twentieth century. For one thing, the whole project wouldn't have been possible without the military and logistical assistance the Germans lent the Ottoman Empire: eight hundred German officers were sent to support the Turkish army in the war against Russia and Britain.

Not only that but, as I read with incredulity, Berlin was actively involved in the proclamation of jihad, helping to reinflame the religious hatred against "unbelievers."

With the evolution of a more secular philosophy in the nineteenth century, the concept of holy war had gone somewhat out of fashion. At least, the Ottoman Empire did not wage the Russian-Turkish War or the last Balkan Wars under the banner of jihad. During the First World War, however, the German Empire deliberately sought to provoke such a conflict after Islamic experts in Berlin hatched a plan to mobilize religious fighters in the name of Islam. The diplomat and secret service agent Max von Oppenheim (nicknamed "Abu Jihad," meaning "father of the holy war") proposed a strategy to the German Kaiser whereby

a religious war would be declared in order to incite the
Muslim population in British or Russian territories to rebellion, and so tie up the military power of Germany's enemies.

To this end, the German war propagandists in Berlin
had flyers calling for a holy war printed and distributed
in Istanbul and even Persia. The Berlin Foreign Office
published the weekly paper *Al-Jihad,* and German consu-
lates set up numerous reading rooms in the Ottoman
Empire in order to spread the idea.

At the request of the Germans, the Turkish government
arranged a public proclamation of jihad. Sheik ul-Islam,
the highest theological authority, signed a fatwa, and the
sultan called on Muslims to take part in the great religious
struggle. Henceforward, the blood of unbelievers could be
spilled with impunity. From the minarets, the muezzins
called for the murder of Christians, and white turbans
were worn in the mosques as a sign that a holy war was in
progress.

On November 19, 1914, the green battle flag of the
Prophet Muhammad was unfurled in the Sunni city of
Medina, and the sword of Hussein was carried in a procession in Shiite Karbala. In another bit of propaganda, it
was even rumored around the Ottoman Empire that the
German Kaiser had converted to Islam and was now known
as "Hajji Wilhelm Muhammad."

The famous Dutch Islamic scholar Hurgronje warned
Germany that it was playing with fire: if religious fanaticism
were unleashed again, the native Christians in the Ottoman
Empire would be the first to suffer. Events were to prove him
only too right, as the Muslim population understood the
call to jihad as an all-out war on unbelievers, who must be
forced to adopt Islam. Supported by the German propaganda
machine, a ghastly slaughter of the indigenous Christian

population now began. Alongside the Turks, Kurdish tribal leaders and their clans eagerly followed the call to jihad by looting property and raping women and children. Even the normally sacrosanct principle of hospitality was jettisoned in the holy war, with Kurds taking persecuted Christians into their homes on the pretext of giving them sanctuary, only to stab them to death in cold blood.

American diplomats also reported on the unspeakable cruelty with which Greeks, Arameans, and Armenians were being slaughtered as religious extremism allied itself with the basest social instincts. This barbaric destruction took place with the widespread participation of the Muslim population. Muslims who might otherwise have come to the Christians' aid were dissuaded by laws declaring that anyone who protected Armenians would be executed. Indeed, killing your Armenian friends was regarded as proof of religious allegiance to God.

Through the accounts of its diplomats and military, the German government in Berlin was well informed of what was going on in the Ottoman Empire. But the government closed its eyes to the genocide, and on December 7, 1915, Chancellor Bethmann Hollweg insisted that, "Our sole objective is to keep Turkey on our side until the end of the war, whether the Armenians die or not." To prevent any news of the Christians' annihilation from leaking out, the Berlin Foreign Office hired journalists to engineer a cover-up. And to add to the catalog of shame, even the churches in Germany largely abandoned the Armenians to the clutches of a rabid religious nationalism.

After the First World War, Germany declined to admit to any part in the genocide, and Turkey itself did everything in its power to hush it up. Truth is the first casualty of war, as the saying goes, and the same applies to genocide: having annihilated a whole segment of the population, the perpetrators attempt to obscure, downplay, or deny their crime outright.

In Germany there are, quite rightly, countless memorials to Jewish synagogues and cemeteries, along with commemorative plaques and monuments evoking the Jewish Holocaust. But there is nothing of the kind in Turkey. On the contrary, the state has invested large sums of money in order to discredit historians researching the genocide. All traces have been erased: over ten thousand place names of Armenian origin, along with the names of rivers and mountains, have been obliterated and replaced with Turkish ones. In 1934, all non-Muslims were made to adopt Turkish surnames. Churches were turned into mosques, cattle sheds, or public toilets. Church ruins were used by the Turkish artillery for target practice, and the remaining foundation walls as material for the construction of Turkish houses. The typically Armenian wayside crosses were smashed. Even when "renovating" historic buildings, the Turks were careful to remove any signs of Armenian origin.

While Franz Werfel's novel *The Forty Days of Musa Dagh* did much to bring the destruction of the Armenians to wider public knowledge in Western countries, it was not made into a film for decades due to Turkish intervention. Turkish schoolbooks continue to claim that the genocide is an unfounded allegation. Armenian and Aramaic Christians are branded traitors or barbarians and churches and synagogues are described as "harmful institutions." In 2009, Prime Minister Erdogan asserted that there was not a single document to prove the Armenian genocide, and promised to fight the liars seeking to blacken Turkey's name. Even part of the Turkish intellectual elite still persists in denying the genocide, and the destruction of the remaining Christian cultural assets is seen by many as a cause for jubilation.

In Germany, denial of the Jewish Holocaust is a criminal offence; in Turkey, by contrast, a mere reference to the Armenian genocide is punishable with a five-year jail sentence. When France proposed a bill to recognize the killings officially as genocide, Turkey threatened it with economic sanctions, and the bill was quickly filed away in a drawer. In Germany, the government of the state of Brandenburg yielded to pressure from the Turkish embassy in 2005 and removed a reference to the genocide from the school curriculum. When various governments marked the centenary of the slaughter in 2015, Turkey flew into a rage. In response to Pope Francis's allusion to "genocide," it withdrew its ambassador to the Vatican. Erdogan accused the pope of talking nonsense and encouraging racism in Europe. There were even numerous calls to assassinate the pope.

The argument advanced by some German politicians that the extermination of the Armenians cannot be recognized as "genocide" because the term wasn't defined until 1948 is simply absurd. Has it escaped these people's notice that the destruction of Armenian and Aramaic Christians was the very reason for establishing the UN definition in the first place? In 1921, the Polish-Jewish lawyer and historian Lemkin came across the mass extermination of the Armenians and Aramaic Christians in his research and called it a "barbaric crime." He called for an international law against racial and religious murder and, as early as 1933, submitted a draft convention to that effect to the League of Nations. With great foresight, Lemkin recognized that the mass murder of Armenians and Arameans could be used as a model for other regimes, and that such crimes should therefore be outlawed internationally. And sure enough, when presenting his plans for the extermination of the Jews in

1939, Adolf Hitler posed the question: "Who speaks today of the annihilation of the Armenians?" In 1943, Lemkin coined the term "genocide" for these acts of barbarism and, in 1948, his convention was approved by the UN.

Regardless of all these facts, the German Foreign Office – in view of Turkey's status as a NATO member and economic partner – warned against describing the mass killing of Armenians in 1915 as genocide. Some politicians refused to be silenced, however. The president of the German Bundestag, Norbert Lammert, made it clear that "what happened during the First World War in the Ottoman Empire was a genocide." The politician Norbert Röttgen took a similarly brave stand: "Today we end the silence and secrecy." And finally, on June 2, 2016, the German Bundestag – despite threats from Turkey – passed a resolution recognizing the mass murder of Armenians in the First World War as genocide, and without attempting to conceal the complicity of the German Empire.

Why is Turkey so afraid to face up to its own history? For one thing, it might then be obliged to make reparations, as the Germans have done with respect to Jews and the State of Israel. Secondly, a confession of guilt would constitute a stain upon Turkish honor. Another reason for the Turks' stubborn denial of genocide could well be that the annihilation of the Christian peoples of Asia Minor was in part *religiously motivated*. Coming to terms with it would therefore require an attempt to understand the hatred of Christians that erupts periodically within Islam; it would mean going back to the roots of the barbaric cruelty that runs like a thread through its history. And that critical analysis would have to include the founder of Islam, the Prophet Muhammad, who was himself responsible for the extermination of a Jewish tribe, the Banu Qurayza, ordering the beheading of all able-bodied men and the enslavement of women and children.

This subject, however, is taboo. The Koran and the Prophet Muhammad's example are regarded as sacrosanct; any criticism is construed as an insult to Islam and the Prophet and brutally avenged. But if the example is not allowed to be questioned, there will always be blind imitators. As long as any discussion of the roots of violence is forbidden, it risks being endlessly reproduced. To deny the offence is to remain attached to it.

Turkey's refusal to deal critically with its nationalistic founding is one of the reasons why it has still not found peace to this day, with regard to Kurdish rights, for example. And it's probably fair to say that its persistent denial of the genocide of 1915 is part of the reason why similar crimes are still being repeated – why many Armenians whose ancestors fled to Syria a hundred years ago are now being displaced, again in the name of Islam, by jihadists. On March 21, 2014, a radical Islamic group of the "Syrian opposition" attacked Kassab, a small Syrian town with a majority Armenian population just a few kilometers from Musa Dagh. Once again, Christians in the very region made famous by Franz Werfel's novel were forced to convert to Islam, flee, or risk being murdered.

For the wounds of a crime to heal, it takes an admission of guilt and a plea for forgiveness, in this case to the victims' descendants. There also needs to be a willingness to make amends, even if it comes too late for the dead themselves. Suppression and denial only come back to haunt the offender, leading to a compulsive repetition of the crime. According to a Jewish proverb which set the tone for Germany's handling of the Holocaust legacy, "Remembrance is the secret of redemption." The mechanisms of evil can only be exposed and countered by remembering and reflecting on the wrongs committed. The Christian churches likewise struggled for a long time to admit and come to terms with their role in anti-Semitic violence. In my view, the task of exposing and eliminating the religious aspect of discrimination and violence is the most urgent one facing Islam today.

Many Turkish historians and writers are committed to this task, but they – journalists in particular – often come under pressure if they venture to denounce the misuse of Islamic ideology or point to the atrocities committed against the Armenians, for example. I have noticed recently, to my relief, that Turkey's restrictions on freedom of the press have been closely watched by Western media. And with good reason: the journalists detained in Turkey deserve our solidarity.

Zuvinar shows me pictures of Deir ez-Zor on her phone. First, a completely bombed-out street and, in the midst of it, circled in red, the house she grew up in, now a ruin. Next, a snap of the church erected in memory of the genocide, and at whose consecration Garo and Zuvinar first met.

In Deir ez-Zor, the site of the largest Armenian concentration camp, the events of 1915–16 were commemorated by a church, a monument, and an archive. Human skeletons recovered from the caves were interred under plexiglass and placed on public view. But on September 21, 2014, Deir ez-Zor was captured by IS and the church and memorial were blown up, the date being deliberately chosen to coincide with Armenian Independence Day. I suspect that this action won IS further credit with the Turkish government.

Imagine what an outcry there would be around the world – and rightly so – if the memorial sites of Auschwitz or Yad Vashem were blown up and razed to the ground. How hurtful it must be, then, for Eastern Christians – and particularly for the surviving descendants of those killed in the 1915 genocide – to see the destruction of their own memorial passed over in silence by the global community.

The twelve-year-old Agob tells me that, on his visit to Deir ez-Zor, he went to places where thousands of his ancestors had been slaughtered, and that if you rubbed the grass there between your fingers you could smell the blood.

I refrain from commenting on this last observation; whether or not the grass really smells of blood I don't know. All I know, I think to myself, is that no grass must be allowed to grow over the atrocities of the Armenian genocide.

15

The Death of a Language

"Eli, Eli, lema sabachthani?" When a refugee from Qaraqosh speaks these words, they are not simply quoting from the Bible in a foreign language, but uttering a *cri de coeur* in their native Aramaic: "My God, my God, why have you forsaken me?" And when a father nags his young daughter to get out of bed and go to school, he will say, "Talitha cumi!" (literally, "little girl, I say to you, get up!") – the same words spoken by Jesus when he brought a dead girl back to life. The authors of the New Testament preserved the original expression, handing it down for posterity like a precious linguistic relic, and Jesus' Aramaic mother tongue also became that of many Middle Eastern Christians for centuries.

The Aramaic language still survives to this day in residual Christian enclaves. Until 1915, the largest Aramaic-speaking demographic group lived in a fairly homogenous area in Upper Mesopotamia, extending into the Mosul and Urmia Plain. This area is now part of the tri-border region of Turkey, Iran, and Iraq. The Suryani, as they were known, lived in five hundred or so villages and a few small towns, with a further sizeable population of Aramaic Christians in the city of Mosul. During the First World War, the majority of these Christians – numbering around five hundred thousand – were murdered or displaced. The survivors mostly settled in villages which, following the dissolution of the Ottoman Empire, were distributed between the three states of Turkey, Iran, and Iraq.

In addition to these enclaves, two tiny territories remain within Syria where an Aramaic dialect is still spoken: a few villages in a mountain range to the northeast of Damascus and the "camps" on the Khabur River.

Until recently, in short, there were five areas left where the language survived in one form or another, but even these linguistic treasures are now being forcibly extinguished, like five lights going out one by one. And with the language goes an age-old Christian culture. Once again, we are witnessing a countdown to annihilation, as diversity gives way to the growing darkness of barbarism:

Five: Tur Abdin, in the southeast of modern-day Turkey, has a barren landscape, more hilly than mountainous, with fertile valleys running through it. Toward the south, the high plateau falls away sharply, giving a view across to the broad plains of Mesopotamia. The name "Tur Abdin" means "mountain of the servants (of God)," and refers to the many hermits who once eked out a meager and precarious existence in this ancient Christian territory. In its heyday, Tur Abdin was home to tens of thousands of monks, living in eighty or so monasteries and numerous hermitages, and was renowned for its theological school. During the genocide of 1915–16, some thirty thousand Aramaic-speaking Christians were slaughtered, including all the monks at the famous – and oldest – monastery of Mar Gabriel.

Around 1960, the surviving Christian population numbered approximately two hundred thousand, although many of the Aramaic-speaking villages in and around the area had become forcibly Islamized or – following the expulsion of their Christian inhabitants – dominated by Kurds. More recently, the Aramaic Christians became caught up in the war waged by Turkish government troops against

Kurdish rebels. Violence and persistent discrimination made life increasingly unbearable for the traditionally unarmed Christians. The Turkish courts did nothing to prosecute the abduction and forced Islamization of girls or the murder of Christians. The vast majority of the original population emigrated and became dispersed throughout Europe, America, and Australia, so that their language, culture, and Syriac Christian customs have been all but lost.

The Christian population of the Tur Abdin area is down to roughly two thousand and dropping, with no end in sight, short of annihilation. There are just six monasteries left, including the great Mar Gabriel. A small ray of hope emerged in 2001 when Turkish Prime Minister Bülent Ecevit invited Aramaic Christians to return to their homeland. But this turned out to be highly problematic in practice, as Kurds had by now occupied most formerly Christian homes and continued to terrorize the last of their Christian neighbors. Since then, the political winds have turned again in favor of Islamization and Christian persecution, as the 2015 election campaign showed.

On a visit to Germany in 2010, Turkish Prime Minister Erdogan insisted that forced assimilation of Muslims is "a crime against humanity." Erdogan rightly called for protection of the Turkish Muslim minority in Germany, yet the Turkish government simultaneously discriminates against the Christian minority in Turkey, which – largely as a result of the 1915 genocide – has dwindled from over 20 percent of the population to a fraction of a percent. The remaining few continue to be harassed by measures such as the ban on the training of priests and on the construction or renovation of churches. Not a single church has been built in Turkey since 1923. Worse still, some of the remaining few were taken over by the state as recently as 2016.

A few years ago, the monastery of Mar Gabriel was forced to go to court over the seizure of its property. When Aramaic Christians around the world attempted to draw attention to the 1915–16 genocide, the authorities stepped up the coercive pressure on the monastery, seeking to blot out the memory of past injustice with more of the same.

More recently, the monastery has had to defend itself against widespread rumors that its church was built on the foundations of a mosque; therefore, the argument goes, the church should be demolished and the mosque rebuilt. The church actually dates back to the year 397, centuries before the emergence of Islam, yet local Turkish authorities continue to stir up the dispute in a bid to drive the last remaining Aramaic Christians from their ancestral homeland.

Four: The last Aramaic communities in Iran are currently living – or rather dying – on the *Urmia Plain,* near the Turkish-Iraqi border. In 1960, Persia was still home to around sixty thousand Arameans, and in 1968 a Franciscan community set up a small branch there. Luca, one of the friars, has kept a diary over the years, which he offers to share with me. It gives a first-hand impression of the life of Christians in Iran:

Shirabad, October 20, 1968

The village of Shirabad, where we have been living for a few weeks now, is set in an idyllic landscape: to the east, we look out over the still waters of the vast Lake Urmia, and to the west, across to the tall, proud peaks of Kurdistan separating us from Turkey. I feel like I have been transported back to a biblical age: the houses are made of clay and the women fetch water from the well in jugs. Since our arrival, we have been attempting to learn the language of the villagers – the same language that Jesus learned on Mary's knee. The best way to do this is by working alongside the locals, so we offer ourselves as casual laborers, helping with house building, on fruit farms, in vineyards, and with the grain harvest. That way, we seek to share in the lives of the people and cultivate their friendship.

There are another thirty or so small villages in this area that are home to Aramaic Christians, also known as Chaldeans here. There are probably around six thousand Christian inhabitants in total, but their number is constantly falling. Why? Because they feel like strangers here, even though it has been their home for many centuries. And the more that leave, the harder it becomes for those left behind.

Politically speaking, there is a relatively high degree of religious tolerance. But in everyday life, Christians are made to feel that they don't belong and have no right to be here. According to estimates, there are only forty thousand Chaldeans left in the whole of Persia, many of them living in the big cities such as Tehran, where they find work, but at the expense of their language and culture. In Shirabad too, Christian culture is disappearing due to the dearth of church services and means of communicating religious knowledge available to such a small Christian community. Grandparents still know their Bible inside out – it's their world – but the next generation has lost these roots. Our goal is to refamiliarize them with their own faith through Bible discussions and religious education.

Shirabad, December 18, 1984

Since the Iranian Revolution five years ago, we have been inundated with Muslim propaganda promoting a fanatical approach to Islam. Christian children have to learn an Islamic catechism at school, and we hear on the television that pigs and non-Muslims are unclean. Even the simple villagers sense a more aggressive atmosphere when they come to Urmia for their shopping, for example. Old memories are coming back to haunt people, such as the murder of five thousand worshippers in the church square in 1918, including two bishops and fifteen priests; or the thirty thousand Aramaic Christians who fled to Urmia before the massacres and died there from hunger and disease. Yes, there are friendships between Muslims and Christians. But now Christians are worried that a potential persecutor may lurk within the friend, ready to resurface at any moment. . . . As a Christian, it's almost impossible to find a job anymore. At school, Christianity is presented in a bad light in many subjects, from history to literature. Christian children are not allowed to drink from the same faucet as their Muslim schoolmates. And in a downpour, a Christian may not take shelter in a Muslim house, otherwise it will be rendered impure. A Christian is, quite simply, of lesser value. If a Christian is killed in a car accident, for example, insurers will pay out just 10 percent of what they would pay in the case of a Shiite. We no longer have the right to print our own newspapers, and even photocopied hymn sheets for our church services are censored. Recently, one of these was rejected because it contained the expression "Son of God." Wherever they go, local Christians are made to feel they no longer belong; they are like fish out of water.

Shirabad, October 15, 1988

A young Christian, thirty years old, was accused of having sex with a Muslim woman, a crime punishable by death. He was imprisoned and tortured for nearly two years. The alternative offered him according to the law was very tempting: all he had to do was become a Muslim, and he would be free to go. But the man refused to enter into this unfair bargain. I was able to visit him in the days before his hanging, and was deeply impressed by the spiritual path he had chosen. He wanted to stay true to his faith, even praying for those who had condemned him unjustly.

The service held in his memory was very moving; he was celebrated by the Christians here as a martyr from their ranks. The history of their church, their liturgy, and their whole attitude to life and spirituality are marked by martyrdom.

What was extraordinary about that day was that, in an environment where all the talk is of revenge – for those killed in the war against Iraq, for the victims of the attacks, and even for the tiniest things – in a world where political propaganda is constantly sowing hatred, and even the law is framed in a spirit of revenge, the small Christian community chooses the path of forgiveness. Not out of helplessness, because they are unable to exact revenge, but quite deliberately, as a specifically Christian stance, bearing witness to the forgiveness of Christ. The service and the whole atmosphere of these last few days have shaken me to the core. I feel like I am living on an island of peace in the midst of an unpacific ocean.

Reading this diary, it strikes me that although a language may be dying, this message of forgiveness and reconciliation must not be allowed to die. In a conversation via Skype, Luca tells me that, as of 2016, there is only one Christian family left in Shirabad among 220 Muslim families (fifty years ago it was home to sixty-five Chaldean families and one Muslim family). All other Aramaic villages are now occupied exclusively by Kurds; the churches are decaying and mosques are being built in their place. The only remaining Chaldean Christians are in large cities, and even there their number has fallen to below ten thousand. After a presence of nearly two thousand years, the Chaldeans will soon be gone forever. One Chaldean bishop remains in

Urmia, but he will probably be the last, his main mission being to administer the last rites to the old Arameans who have remained.

This has to be done in Aramaic, as Christian priests in Iran are strictly forbidden to preach in Persian, the national language, even though it has long become the everyday tongue of city-dwelling Christians. Presumably, the mullahs fear that their followers might be seduced by the Christian message. Consequently, the last Aramaic Christians are compelled by the state to farewell the dying in their own, dying language.

Three: I have already talked about the fate of the Iraqi city of *Qaraqosh.* Here and in the surrounding villages, Aramaic was still spoken until the IS occupation of August 2014 – in fact a dedicated university had been planned for this still-large demographic group of the Nineveh Plain. That hope, however, has been dashed by IS.

Two: Since 1934, many mountain Assyrians displaced from the Hakkari region have settled in *thirty-four villages along the Khabur River in Syria.* For decades, the Syrian state offered a last refuge for many Christians from Turkey, Iran, or Iraq. But then the maelstrom of political events swept Syria, too, into a murderous civil war whose main beneficiaries have been radical Islamic groups, allowing the Islamic State, for example, to conquer large areas and subject them to its ruthless diktat.

Among the Christian refugees who have ended up in Leipzig are a few from one of the villages on the Khabur. Thanks to Yousif's networking, I get to know one such family, and come face to face with the misery of these people on my very first visit.

Isaak is clearly a disturbed child. He hides behind the table,
stealing the odd glance in my direction. I try to draw him
out with a smile, but to no avail. The four-year-old must
have been through some traumatic experiences. His father
Nabil also shows signs of severe emotional strain; he talks
terribly loudly, and the fact that I don't understand a word
probably makes him sound even louder to my ears. Yousif
relays the gist of the newly arrived Syrian refugee's words.
Like his son, Nabil is hard to make eye contact with, and
comes across as highly tense and nervous. Nabil's native
tongue is Aramaic, but he also speaks Arabic. The original
reason for my visit today was to fill out Isaak's kindergarten
registration form, with Yousif's help. But only a few hours
ago, Nabil received news that his brother, sister-in-law, and
their three children have drowned off the Turkish coast.
Nabil's wife, Lilian, sits on the sofa in a daze and starts
to cry again. I feel powerless to help in such a horrendous
situation. Yousif, too, sits in silence, staring at the picture
on Nabil's smartphone of the little boat – a tiny cockleshell
that was to have ferried eighteen Syrian refugees across to a
Greek island. Nabil's brother had sent the picture today, just
before the crossing. How cruel to have narrowly escaped
death in their home country only to die at sea!

Nabil and his family are originally from the Syrian town
of Tel Tamer, where his grandfather settled in 1934 to build
a new future for himself. In this semi-arid region on the
Khabur River, the refugees established thriving villages,
built schools and churches, and created a new home for
themselves. But, once again, their peace was short-lived: on
February 23, 2015, IS began its assault on the villages. Nabil
just managed to escape with Lilian and little Isaak, making
their way to Germany via a hazardous route through Turkey
and Greece. Following an initial stay in an asylum seeker
hostel, they have now moved into a small apartment in

Leipzig-Grünau. The rest of the family are still stuck in refugee camps. Or on their way to Europe. Or drowned.

When IS forces invaded the Christian villages, they began by murdering a teacher and a doctor before taking nearly three hundred Christians hostage. First, the hostages were told that if they wanted to be released, they must adopt Islam. To drive home this message, fifteen young men were executed, and the most attractive women were taken to be shared among the militants' leaders. For all the other hostages, a ransom was fixed. In a letter to the Bishop of Hassake, Aprem Athnil, IS demanded fifty thousand dollars per hostage. This placed the bishop in a terrible moral dilemma, knowing the money would be used to continue funding terrorism against Christians. He also got into financial difficulty, and was only able to purchase the release of a few of the hostages. The fate of more than two hundred Christians still in IS custody remains in the balance even now.

In the meantime, IS has laid waste to some of the villages which had been home to the persecuted Christians for eighty years, demolishing their churches and desecrating the graves in the cemetery. Even since the removal of IS and recapture of the territory, some of the Christian houses have been looted or occupied by the (German armed and trained) Kurdish troops. Thus another Christian area is being violently destroyed, and its Aramaic-speaking inhabitants are now dispersed around the world.

One: Many years ago, I had the opportunity of visiting *Ma'loula*, another Aramaic enclave. The journey there and my experiences in this ancient Christian village left a deep impression on me.

It was August, and the heat was unbearable. How could anyone be crazy enough to pedal across the Syrian desert when it was 113 degrees *in the shade?* Or would have been, if there were any shade. At least the airstream cooled us a little, and the people by the roadside spurred us on with an encouraging wave.

That was in the summer of 1995, when I traveled with four friends from Istanbul to Jerusalem. From Homs, we cycled southward in the blazing heat through a scorched desert landscape. I'll never forget the time we stopped, exhausted, outside a random house on the highway and asked, with much waving of hands, if we could put our tent up in the adjacent field. We were met with a charming smile and a welcoming gesture, and our two mosquito tents were barely erected before our Muslim host appeared again, beckoning to us to follow him. He showed us five made-up beds and explained to us with his few words of English that we had the choice of roughing it on the hard ground or sleeping in a proper bed. It didn't take much thinking about, and we enjoyed not only a comfortable night's rest but an ample, tasty supper as well.

Thus fortified, we set off again the next morning ready to tackle the Qalamun Mountains northeast of Damascus. Late in the afternoon, we approached Ma'loula, a village nestling in a narrow gorge between two peaks. According to legend, when Saint Thecla adopted Christianity her father flew into a rage and had her followed. Thecla fled into the mountains, which opened up to create an escape route for her, hence the name "Ma'loula," which means "entrance" in Aramaic.

We pushed our bikes up the picturesque narrow streets, climbing higher and higher until we reached the Convent of Saint Thecla, which sits huddled, as if for protection, beneath the mighty rock face. Then we pulled long trousers and

decent shirts over our cycling gear and entered the ancient
sanctuary, which felt refreshingly cool after our hot climb.

Inside, we plunged into a mystical twilight penetrating
the interior through the domes. A few incense clouds
hovered on the air, making the light visible and filling the
space with a heady, exotic scent. I stood under a crystal
chandelier looking up into the light filtering through the
dome windows.

Then I sat down in a pew, planting my feet consciously on
the ancient ground on which the Christian faith has thrived
for nearly two thousand years. The icons glowed mesmeriz-
ingly in the candlelight, the gold-backed saints looking back
at me with large eyes. In my mind, I was transported back
through the centuries to the dawn of Christianity. Even if
Saint Thecla's conversion by Paul the Apostle belongs to the
realm of legend, it reminded me of the significant role of
women in early Christianity.

While I was sitting there, a woman entered the church,
walked up to the chancel, and kissed the icons on either
side. She stood for a while, softly murmuring a prayer.
Although I didn't understand a word, I was moved to hear
her praying in Aramaic, the language of Jesus. It was like
going back in time, connecting me to the source of Christianity and to Jesus himself.

Even this thin, continuous thread leading back to
the origins of Christianity was severed by the jihadists.
On December 3, 2013, fighters from the Al-Nusra Front
abducted twelve nuns from the convent; shortly after, they
captured Ma'loula and other small Christian towns, dese-
crated the churches, and burned the icons. The message was
clear: Christians, get out of our territory!

This time no mountains parted to give refuge. Men
with Christian-sounding names who weren't prepared to
adopt Islam were executed. The entire village of Kanaye

was forcibly converted under threat of a bloodbath. In the ancient Christian town of Sadat, forty-five men, women, and children were tortured, killed, and buried in a mass grave. The religious fighters had also taken some young men prisoner in Ma'loula with a view to converting them. One of the men refused, and was shot before his friends' eyes. How the others, who "converted" after witnessing this brutal act, must have felt – the fear, doubt, and shame that must have haunted them – one can only imagine. Yet even the capture and destruction of Ma'loula, a village with such a venerable Christian tradition, received scant coverage in the Western press.

Since then, the abducted nuns have been released and Ma'loula has been recaptured by the Syrian army, but there is still no sign of six young men who were kidnapped at the time. Many houses lie in ruins and the portals of the ancient churches are charred. The church furnishings have been smashed and the icons stolen or torn to pieces. The scent of incense now mingles with the smell of burning.

Whether Mosul or Tur Abdin, Damascus or Ma'loula, these places where the *first* Christians once gathered and prayed in Aramaic might now be inhabited by the *last* Christians to do so. I am reminded of an Aramaic expression, a cry for help uttered by the oppressed early Christians: "Maranatha!" – "Come, O Lord!"

16

Through a Child's Eyes

In September 2015, after my summer vacation, I pay a visit
to Yousif's family. Amanuel and Shaba have been attending
a Christian school in Leipzig since the beginning of term,
and I want to find out how they're getting on. After a bit of
small talk about the holidays, Amanuel asks whether I know
about the refugees found dead in a truck in Austria. Having
heard very little news on vacation, I only know about the
incident from the headline: "71 Bodies in Death Truck."
Amanuel wants to tell me more, and shows me a photo on
his phone of the inside of a truck containing a huge pile of
corpses. I am instantly reminded of the gruesome images
from Nazi concentration camps, of mountains of bodies
with arms, hands, and legs sticking out in all directions, the
only difference being that the bodies in the truck are fully
clothed.

Shaba moves closer to look at the picture. I turn away,
appalled. "You shouldn't look at such horrible pictures."

Shaba replies slowly and calmly. "Andreas, I've seen much
worse than that. And not just pictures, I mean real life."

I swallow. What traumas these children have already
been through! I remember an occasion shortly after we
first met. Yousif was anxious to tell me what had befallen a
Christian village in his homeland, and got the ten-year-old
Shaba to translate for him: "And then the Islamic State

people cut the child's head off." Hearing such words from the mouth of a little girl was almost unbearable.

In the fall, Amanuel went on a school trip and found himself sitting around the campfire with his classmates one evening. For the German students, the bonfire held a strong fascination, conjuring up associations of adventure and romance; for Amanuel, it stirred up very different emotions. He began to describe the houses and whole streets he had seen go up in flames in Iraq, and how people ran for their lives, crying for help. The whole class sat mesmerized, listening to the horrors that Amanuel needed to get out of his system. "I know what war is. Be glad that you don't."

"I've seen bodies on the street," he continued. "Severed hands and feet and heads. All covered in blood. War is hideous."

The other children fell quiet when they heard this, and some began to cry.

"I've seen too much," Amanuel says to me now. "I've deleted all the pictures of burning houses on my phone, but I can't delete them from my head."

Like me, Amanuel's homeroom teacher noticed that he had developed a nervous facial twitch. We arranged an appointment with a neurologist, who concurred that the cause of this physical symptom was likely the harrowing images imprinted indelibly on his mind. When he was barely eight, for example, he had run into a group of people on the way home from school. All of a sudden, a young man with bound limbs was forced to his knees right beside him. Two men in black masks held the victim down while a third began to cut off his head with a long knife. Amanuel stared, petrified, at the act taking place directly before his eyes.

"Have you ever seen anything like this?" he asks me, holding out his phone. I shake my head emphatically, waving it away with both hands. Only recently, I read in a book about IS that the perpetrators hack away for about thirty seconds when beheading their victims, causing blood to gush everywhere. The last thing I want to do is to watch an Islamic State propaganda video where this barbaric act is celebrated as a religious rite.

Amanuel had been forced to witness such a terrible thing *live*. It wasn't until the executioner held the severed head aloft, dripping with blood, with a cry of "Allahu akbar!" that Amanuel roused himself from his state of shock and ran off in a blind panic. He arrived home crying and sobbing with terror. For a long time, he couldn't speak about what he had seen. For days he was completely traumatized and unable to sleep at night. Even today, his dreams are sometimes haunted by the images that have etched themselves on his memory and soul, perhaps forever.

I am reminded of Isaak, who has been attending kindergarten for the last few months. The head teacher invited his father, Nabil, and me for a chat. "Sometimes," she said, "Isaak just stares at the floor and shuts off; or he crawls under the table or under a blanket." She was clearly a sensitive person, and wanted to know whether Isaak was like this at home too and, if so, how his parents reacted. "Should I just leave him alone when that happens? Or is it better to engage with him?"

Nabil explained that the boy was the same at home, and that he and Lilian simply waited until he came around again before trying to talk to him.

"What's made him like this?" the teacher inquired.

Nabil explained what life had been like in Tel Tamer: "When Lilian was pregnant with Isaak and went into labor,

I took her to the small hospital in the next town. Just as we were leaving the house, a car bomb exploded nearby and knocked us to the ground. All the panes in our house were shattered. We were terrified of another bomb exploding. I supported my wife, who was shaking all over, and we ran as fast as we could to a friend's house, and he drove us to the hospital."

Deeply shaken, the teacher and I remained silent for a while. And when Nabil went on to speak of the growing terror at home, their flight over land and sea, the fragmentation of his family, and the friends still being held hostage by IS, it became clear what deep-seated anxieties little Isaak must have been encumbered with as a small child, and even before his birth.

Then came the time at the asylum seeker hostel. Nabil's account of the lack of solidarity shown toward Christians by fellow refugees matched the experiences of other families I have spoken to. I was particularly shocked to hear tales of Christians being thrown overboard by Muslim refugees. One would have thought that they were – literally – in the same boat. But the contempt toward Christians runs so deep that the human solidarity instinct sometimes fails to kick in. This even applies to Muslim children who have settled in Germany; they simply repeat what they have learned at home. And so the hatred of Christians implanted in the minds of Muslims for generations continues to bear its poisonous fruit. Thus little Isaak was regularly taunted, bullied, and sometimes even beaten by the other children at the hostel for being a "pork eater" and "unclean."

I had heard similar tales from Amanuel and Shaba, who had both had a lot to deal with in their German school. Even in this country, the small silver cross Amanuel proudly wore around his neck had landed him in trouble. Spotting it, an older Muslim boy had begun calling him names, then pretended to point a machine gun at him: "Ratatatata! Shoot the Christians!" Complaints to the principal were to no avail. Fortunately, both children were able to switch to a church school, where they are treated with respect and consideration – Amanuel has even been elected class representative.

Authorities and politicians are often loath to admit to the bullying of Christians by their Muslim co-residents in asylum seeker hostels. And a large number of cases presumably go unreported due to threats and intimidation. This problem has been highlighted by the German police union, which has proposed segregation of Christians and Muslims. The counterargument of the political establishment is that Muslims need to learn tolerance. But such a deep-rooted anti-Christian mindset, inculcated by decades of preaching, is hardly going to be erased just by crossing a border, attending an integration course, or signing a set of house rules committing to respectful behavior.

Western politicians' responses to discrimination, kidnapping, and murder in Muslim countries often follows the same rationale – the suffering of countless people is ignored because their governments have signed the Universal Declaration of Human Rights.

What effect has all this had on Amanuel and Shaba's psychology? Will these children ever be able to sleep peacefully? And what happens if they encounter fresh violence here in Germany – if the refugee shelters are set alight here too, and black-masked figures begin to parade through the streets shouting hate slogans?

These are not the only worries that refugee children have to contend with. There are other very different challenges facing them, not least helping their parents – who are slower to learn German – to decipher official correspondence or purchase travel tickets. In this way, the normal roles are reversed, with children assuming responsibility for their parents, explaining things they don't understand, accompanying them on visits to the authorities, and interpreting at job interviews. Their childhood has already been stolen from them by the terror in Syria or Iraq and their enforced exile, yet even here in Germany they are still not free to be children, but burdened with the task of looking after their parents.

I remember visiting Yousif and Tara one day when they both burst into tears of grief at the thought of the parents Tara had left behind, and it fell to little Shaba to comfort them. What a heavy load for a little girl to take upon her fragile shoulders!

A few days after my return from Kurdistan, I find a message on my answering machine. It is Amanuel, wanting to speak to me urgently, and asking me to call him back. When I get him on the line, he tells me that others in his sports group suspect him of being a jihadist. I can hear how upset Amanuel is, and fetch my bike from the basement. It's already after eight and I'm tired, but I have a feeling that Amanuel really needs me right now.

Yousif and Tara aren't at home. Shaba joins us on the sofa and I ask Amanuel to tell me the story. He explains that they had decided to hold a minute's silence during the sports lesson in memory of the victims of the Paris terror attack. Two girls had started to talk about how scared they were. The images in the news had left their mark on the children, who were afraid that radical Muslims might launch an attack in Germany too. One boy cited a newspaper headline: "Jihadist Came to France as Refugee," and some of them turned to look at Amanuel.

"Surely you don't think I'm a jihadist!" he choked, going hot and cold all over.

"No, we don't think that," one girl replied after some hesitation.

But Amanuel was conscious of an atmosphere of suspicion and mistrust. He felt cornered and wanted to defend himself: "You can ask Brother Andreas – he knows me. I'm not a jihadist!"

I try to reassure Amanuel, who has worked himself up into quite a state. I feel sorry that this boy, whose family lost their home to jihadists and suffered so much on their account, should now be suspected as a potential jihadist himself.

Six-year-old Abdel Massih has also lived through the war. He is from Aleppo, and lost his father, Jad, there. The name Abdel Massih, as I eventually learn, means "servant of Christ."

Until recently, Aleppo ranked as the Middle Eastern city with the second-largest Christian population, after Mosul. Jad was a goldsmith who had been successful enough to open two branch stores in addition to his own boutique. The family was well off financially and active in the Greek Orthodox community of their home city. Then the dark shadow of the Syrian civil war reached Aleppo. The western part of the city was taken by the IS fighters, while the eastern part was held by President Assad's troops. The Christian quarter in the old town was sandwiched between the two. Jad could have left Syria right at the start of the civil war by virtue of his family connections in Germany, but he didn't want to. "This is my home. And all wars come to an end eventually." Soon afterward, he was to pay for that decision with his life.

The Islamists directed their heaviest fire at the Christian quarter, which formed a buffer zone between them and their opponents. On Good Friday, a street procession is traditionally held in this part of town. The IS terrorists waited for that precise moment to launch their grenades, unleashing a horrific bloodbath. A few weeks later, a teenager was severely wounded in a further attack. He lay on the street in his own blood, crying out in pain. Jad and his brother rushed out of the goldsmith's store to help the boy, and at that moment the next grenade struck, killing Jad and ten other people. Jad's brother was seriously injured and died a few hours later in the hospital.

It was clear to Jad's wife, Myriam, that as a single woman she could no longer stay in Aleppo, and in fall 2014, she and her four children managed to obtain a place on Germany's refugee reception program through the German embassy in Beirut.

In February 2015, I went to Berlin with Rahima, one of Myriam's nieces, to welcome the family to Germany. Rahima had been living in Germany for a long time, and the two women hadn't seen each other for four years. When they met in the arrivals area of the airport, they clutched each other in a long embrace, sobbing loudly. A customs official brought them a pack of tissues. What a reunion! The last time the women had met had been in Aleppo, in more peaceful times; Jad's business was doing well, they had been able to afford a nice home, buy a car, and send all four children to school. Now all that was destroyed.

On the journey from Berlin to Leipzig I learned that neither Myriam nor her three daughters or Abdel Massih had ever flown before, and that, apart from the trip to Beirut, this was the first time they had ever been to another country. It was raining and they all looked out at the grey sky, which made the vast pine forests look drab and colorless.

For the first few months, the five of them were taken
in by a Protestant convent. The sisters received us in their
Sunday best with a welcome song and a freshly baked cake.
Everyone there was moved to tears at meeting a family
who, only a few days before, had been exposed to constant
shelling and barrel bomb explosions. Abdel Massih talked
about the grenades, his aunt translating for him.

"There are always two bangs: one when the grenade is
launched and one when it hits."

I felt uneasy listening to the little boy's talk of grenades,
knowing that one had killed his father. Perhaps this was his
way of dealing with the horror of it all.

His next words made me even more uncomfortable:
"Boom, boom! That's what the music of Aleppo sounds like."

We looked at each other awkwardly. Fortunately, one of
the sisters chose this moment to ask how they wanted to
divide up the two rooms.

I conferred with the sisters about what we could do, particularly for the children. We contacted the neighboring
parish, where the children were soon assimilated into
various groups. Tara and Yousif's children have been similarly welcomed by Christian youth groups, and have even
joined the team of altar servers. It is important that Christian children from Iraq and Syria get the chance to be part
of a community with others of their own age who share the
same faith. It can be challenging for children to protect the
precious legacy of their religion in a secular environment.

Here church schools can also play a role, by offering
refugee children the chance to grow up in a Christian
setting. If, as in Leipzig, schools take children from several
Syrian and Iraqi families, those children will interact and
be better able to preserve their heritage. In this way, church

schools could make it their mission to reach out to Christian children from the Middle East.

A couple of weeks later, I visit the convent again, and one of the sisters tell me the following story. She was out in the grounds with Abdel Massih when they suddenly heard a rescue helicopter. The boy instinctively started, ducked his head, and crouched down. Although at first she didn't know what was wrong with him, it dawned on her that for months or years he must have associated the sound of approaching planes or helicopters with an imminent bombing raid. Over the years, the thump of a helicopter had imprinted itself on the little boy's mind as a harbinger of death and destruction. She helped him to his feet, gave him a hug, and stroked his hair, whispering "Don't be afraid, Abdel Massih. This helicopter isn't going to drop any bombs. It's coming to help someone."

Gradually, Abdel Massih is regaining inner peace. In the convent's spacious gardens, the children can play freely without fear. The sisters keep sheep on the grounds, and I see the children petting some newborn lambs. It's a picture of peace and healing: children who were unable to leave their houses or play outside for months on end, who were torn from their sleep at night by bombs and who have lost their fathers through shellfire, are playing happily with the lambs.

17

Blessed Are the Meek

An uncle of Abdel Massih has arrived in Germany, bringing another tale of blood and tears. Fadi was reluctant to leave Aleppo, and above all his father, who suffered from a heart condition. But the lives of his wife and daughter were at stake, and even his sick father urged him to flee. With the aid of smugglers, the three of them managed to make their way through Turkey before boarding a flimsy dinghy that was to take them across to a Greek island. As they approached the island, the engine died and the men had to drag the boat ashore, swimming through the icy water.

Then came the next hurdle: the smugglers had organized air tickets to Frankfurt and fake Spanish passports, but the fraud was uncovered at customs after a Spanish-speaking border official was called over. When Fadi failed to understand the questions put to him in Spanish, the family's passports were confiscated. Luckily, the smugglers proved reliable and resourceful, and procured fake French passports for them instead. This time it worked. (Fadi says he knows someone who finally got through on his eleventh passport.)

Once again, I fetch a family of three from Berlin in our community's VW bus and take them to the Protestant convent, where Myriam is overjoyed to see her brother and his family again. Fadi still cuts a youthful figure despite his thinning hair. He tells me that he had a good job as a mechanical engineer in Aleppo. He hasn't given up hope of returning, and has kept the key to his apartment in Aleppo, just two hundred yards from the IS-controlled district. So far his apartment block has escaped the bombs and grenades.

"If the war is over soon, I want to go back home," Fadi tells me. "But if the terror goes on for another ten years, I doubt there'll be any chance."

Then, drawing on a religious image, he adds, "After Lent comes Easter, when Jesus rose from the dead. A day will come when the war is over and we can celebrate the resurrection of Syria. That's my hope."

A few days later, I pay another visit to the Protestant convent. Myriam and her sister-in-law have prepared a Middle Eastern supper as a token of thanks to the nuns and myself. Before the meal is served, Fadi proposes a game he has prepared as an ice-breaker. There are two different hats: all the Germans take a piece of paper from the red one, and all the Syrians from the black one. Written on each piece of paper in both German and Arabic is one half of a Bible verse, such as "Blessed are the meek . . ." or "Do not repay evil with evil . . ." The object of the "game" is to find the person with the other half. The German-Syrian pair then discuss their Bible quotation and say something about it to the group at the end, in two languages.

It proves to be a great way of getting us into conversation despite our linguistic difficulties, and we muddle through with much hand waving. The girls have already had a few English lessons back in Aleppo, which helps to oil the wheels of communication.

When the buzz of chatter dies down, we return to the circle and I read the complete verse in German: "Blessed

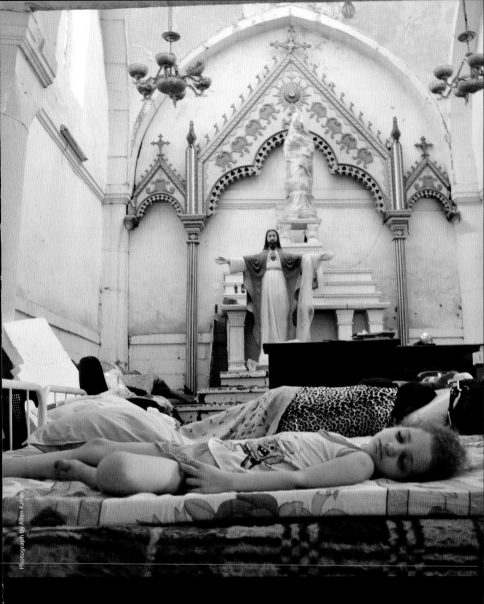

A camp for internally displaced people and refugees in Ankawa, Iraq

Christians displaced by violence taking refuge in Holy Spirit Church, Tel Keppe, Iraq

Displaced Christians living in an unfinished shopping mall in Ankawa.

Refugee camp on the grounds of Mar Elya Church, Ankawa, Iraq

Photograph by Allen Kakony

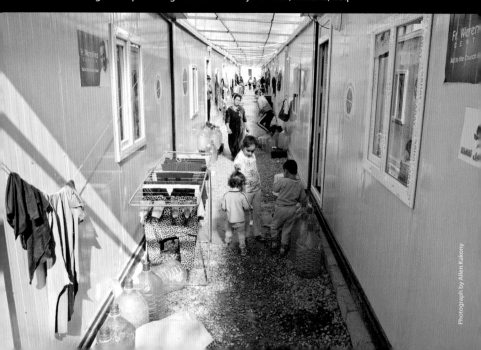

Photograph by Allen Kakony

Passing out bottled water to Christians fleeing Qaraqosh

The destroyed dome of the Church of Saints Sergius and Bacchus in Ma'loula, Syria

The author and two Little Sisters of Jesus visiting a family from Qaraqosh who now live in a single room in Ankawa

Photograph by Allen Kakony

A Good Friday service in a refugee camp in Ankawa

are the meek, for they will inherit the earth." Then Myriam
reads it in Arabic and we both sum up in a couple of
sentences what our quotation means to us, before listening
to the verses and commentaries of the others.

Recognizing a pattern in the verses Fadi has chosen, I
grow thoughtful: they are all about forgiveness, nonviolence, and loving one's enemy. These people have just lost
a husband, father, and uncle to terrorists and been robbed
of their home and possessions – and yet, instead of uttering
words of revenge or retaliation, here they are quoting words
of peace from Jesus' Sermon on the Mount. It amazes me
that people who have suffered such terrible violence can still
pray for their enemies and speak of forgiveness.

A couple months later, Fadi and his family attend the
service organized by my community at our lodgings. The
Bible reading tells the story of the burning bush where
Moses takes off his sandals and learns the name of God: "I
am who I am" (Exod. 3:14).

My fellow brother Gianluca has produced a sheet with
a list of different names for God – creator, shepherd, king,
friend, father, mother, rock, refuge, avenger, etc. – the idea
being that each person reads out the name he likes best.

Fadi uses his smartphone to find translations for words
he doesn't know. Suddenly, he pipes up with the objection
that "avenger" is not a name for God. Gianluca points out
that it appears in the Old Testament. But Fadi insists that,
since the coming of Jesus of Nazareth, we can no longer use
the term "avenger" for God.

Once again I am astonished at this spiritual attitude from
people who have been through such hardship – and who
have lived for centuries in a cultural environment where
revenge and retaliation play a central role. I wonder how

these Christians have managed to avoid being infected by
the notion of holy war and religiously motivated violence.

On another visit, I ask Fadi how they reacted to the
violence they experienced in Aleppo. Fadi is trying hard to
learn German but is still struggling, so Rahima translates
my question: "When you were threatened by the terrorists,
or your brother-in-law was killed, how did you respond?"

There is a brief flash of fire in Fadi's eyes. "If only
we could fight back!" he answers, miming the action of
shooting a gun. Then he shakes his head. "But we are
forbidden." He points to heaven with a single word, "Jesus."

I understand: their loyalty to Jesus prevents them from
retaliating or using force. But I want to know more, so I
pretend not to have caught on. Fadi searches on his smartphone for the translation of an Arabic word, then reads it
aloud to me: "We are pa-ci-fists." I am sure he has never
uttered this foreign word before. In answer to my ques-
tioning look, he reads out further suggested translations for
his Arabic word: "peace-loving; peaceable."

I ask, "Don't Christians in Syria ever use weapons?"

Rahima translates Fadi's response, "Yes, some of us did
military service or worked for the police. That's a civic duty.
In the north of Syria there are Christian villages along
the Turkish border, and the people there have weapons to
defend their property because there are often burglaries and
break-ins."

I nod. Fadi continues: "But they use those weapons as
citizens – not in the name of religion."

Preoccupied as I am with the question of nonviolence,
I ask Yousif too: "What's the attitude of Christians in Iraq
toward weapons and violence?"

"We reject the use of arms. When my uncle was called
up for military service, he suffered terribly. He was sent
directly to the front in the war against Iran, but he always

aimed into the distance, asking the Holy Virgin to send the bullet astray."

"Even in the current situation," Yousif adds, "where Christians like us are being driven out of our towns and villages after eighteen or nineteen hundred years, armed resistance is still not an option for us. We have never fought a war here."

In October 2015, the Russian air force begins a series of missions against IS in Syria. A representative of the Russian Orthodox Church welcomes the deployment as a "holy war." Jacques Behnan Hindo, the Syrian archbishop of Hassake-Nisibis, criticizes this statement in the strongest terms: "As Christians, we cannot talk of a holy war – otherwise what difference would there be between radical Muslims and Christians? Instead, we must make it clear that war is always a sin."

Another bishop, Aprem Athnil, the one who looks after the villages on the Khabur River, even writes a letter to the IS leaders stating, "We categorically reject a culture of weapons," and seeking to impress on IS that the Christian church is not in alliance with the Kurdish Workers' Party, or PKK. True, a so-called Christian militia is fighting alongside the PKK to defend or recapture the villages. But although the international press refers to this militia as "Christian," Bishop Aprem protests that it was neither funded nor approved by the church and that there can be no armed force in the name of Christianity.

What we are seeing here is a clear case of press sensationalism. "Muslim militias versus Christian militias" – such simplifications make the world much easier to explain, even if they are far from the whole truth. Clearly, a report on "Christian militias" grabs attention; a sustained tradition of nonviolence in Eastern Christianity is less interesting

to write about. Has anyone even noticed that, despite the
numerous brutal murders of Christian priests in Iraq or
Syria, no imam has ever been shot, beheaded, or crucified
in the name of Christianity? Or that no Christians have
ever blown themselves up in a mosque in retaliation for the
many attacks on Christian churches? If such a thing had
happened even once, in revenge for the thousands of attacks
on Christians, it would have been front-page news. But such
reprisals, media-friendly though they would have been, have
so far not occurred. The adage "if it bleeds it leads" is only
too true; nonviolence is simply not the stuff of headlines.
Refusal to hit back doesn't make a story. IS bombs itself into
the media, while the far more impressive testimony of pacifism fails to make the copy desk. One exception I found was
in a report by a German journalist who "didn't have much
to do with religion" but, having been to Qaraqosh after the
school bus attack, expressed his amazement at "how little
energy these people channel into hatred and vengefulness."

With Yousif, I bore deeper into this attitude to life: "You
have suffered so much. Why don't you meet violence with
violence?"

Without hesitation, Yousif insists, "As Christians, we are
not supposed to bear arms. There were some Christians in
Mosul who owned weapons, or used them for patrolling
cars at the checkpoints of Christian villages. But they
weren't doing that in the name of Christianity. The church
has always been clear that war is Satan's work."

"Is there no such thing as Christian jihad?" I ask, playing
devil's advocate.

Yousif rejects this emphatically: "Only Muslims have
jihad. Our struggle consists of prayer and fasting. Christianity isn't spread by the sword."

After a pause, Yousif adds, "For terrorists, it's an honor to kill people. Shouldn't it be an honor for us as Christians to pray for and show love to our persecutors?"

In a book written by a historian I discover that this attitude of Yousif's pervades the entire history of the Eastern churches – the belief that religion must never be spread by force is what sets Christianity apart from Islam. Interestingly, this difference has come up again and again in Christian-Muslim dialogues, the Christians arguing that a religious message should be carried by the truth of the words, not by the sword.

In 691, Caliph Abd al-Malik asked the patriarch of the Church of the East, Henanisho I, what he thought of Islam. The patriarch replied that it had come to power by the sword, and that a religion that ignores God's command of nonviolence cannot be a true one. This reply aroused such fury in the caliph that he ordered the brave patriarch's tongue to be cut out.

In other dialogues, too, the Christian parties have insisted that religion should not be spread by force. It was on these grounds that the Byzantine emperor Manuel II criticized the Prophet Muhammad, for instance. But will violence win out in the end? In the ninth century, the Muslim theologian Ali al-Tabari (a former Christian) argued somewhat treacherously, in his *Refutation of Christianity*, that a religion cannot survive in the long run without the concept of a holy war. And as far as the Church of the East and even the mighty Byzantium (Constantinople) are concerned, history seems to have proved him right: Islam has triumphed. So has the notion of a violence-free religion lost out?

The relationship between religion and violence continues to absorb me. Human violence clearly has many causes. Fear or deprivation can have a major impact on our potential for aggression, and rivalry is also a key part of the mix, with jealousy and envy often leading to acts of violence.

A particularly fatal mechanism, it seems, is the infectiousness of human violence. A person who resorts to revenge repeats exactly what was done to him – or worse, pays it back with interest. This begins an endless spiral of violence and counterviolence – in short, a vicious cycle. Other contributing factors are social and political systems, which can amplify the human potential for violence, and the same is true of ideological and religious attitudes.

It is a commonplace nowadays to blame religion itself as the firebrand of human history. There is a general suspicion that religious people are more prone to violence. This is reinforced by frequent references to religious wars and, more recently, the terror perpetrated in the name of Islam.

A closer look at history shows, however, that religion has always sought to bring about a culture of peace and understanding. Even Islam itself grew out of the attempt to bring together the estranged tribes of Arabia through the belief in God. The emphasis on God's mercy in the Koran is explicitly intended to promote a spirit of harmony and reconciliation.

In the Bible more particularly, the focus is on overcoming the root causes of human violence. In the Old Testament, we find a notable evolution in the image of God, who is increasingly understood not just as a dispenser of justice, but also, through his mercy, as a bringer of peace and reconciliation. And this is the core of Jesus' message, that the love of God can fill a person's heart to such an extent that they no longer need to assert themselves by force against their fellow human beings. To experience God's generosity is to escape the trap of human rivalry that compels us to measure ourselves constantly against others. Inspired by this belief, Jesus decisively rejects all acts of violence and thoughts of revenge. He preaches a radical pacifism that transcends the old mechanisms of "an eye for an eye and a tooth for a tooth." Evil is to be conquered by love – a love so strong that it is ultimately prepared to endure injustice and suffer violence. Only then can the vicious cycle of violence and counterviolence be overcome.

Jesus himself was unjustly condemned to die on the cross and thus became a victim of human violence. But God endorses Jesus' message by raising him from the dead; in other words, reconciliation and love triumph over hatred and violence.

During the first few centuries of Christianity, the aspect of nonviolence was given great prominence. When the Western church became the established church, however, some theologians began to argue for the use of force for defense in times of war. The original categorical ban on killing was softened. Before long, heretics who deviated from the faith as officially defined were being brutally persecuted.

It even came to the point of military campaigns in the name of Christianity. The Crusades were a complex phenomenon and cannot be understood simply as Christian aggression against Muslims. For one thing, they were also a reaction to previous attacks by Muslim armies on Christian Byzantium, which turned to the West for military assistance in its hour of need. Instead of sending professional soldiers (mercenaries), however, the West mounted religiously motivated campaigns.

When the first Crusaders arrived in Byzantium, the Eastern Christians were horrified to learn that they were going to war in the name of the cross. The Byzantines refused to accept any kind of holy war, whether crusade or jihad. The message of the gospel was unequivocally one of nonviolence – and therefore a soldier who had fallen in a battle could not be revered as a martyr.

One Byzantine emperor, forced into a corner by the Muslim war of conquest, sought to confront the jihadists with similarly death-defying Christians. But he was vehemently opposed by the patriarch Joannes I, who argued that wars may be politically necessary but must not be fought in the name of God. In short, as far as pacifism is concerned, the churches of the East have remained truer to the gospel than those of the West.

During the Crusades, which were fought with great brutality, there were also many instances of persecution of Jews and all-out campaigns against heretics in the West. The battle to suppress divergent theological schools of thought was subsequently aided by the Inquisition, which regarded torture and killing as legitimate means of protecting the church religion. The violence of the Crusades and the Inquisition remain among the worst deviations from the original teaching and practice of Jesus that history has ever seen.

Even if Jesus' message of pacifism has been forgotten or betrayed over the course of the church's history, his original teaching has always remained a bulwark against violence in the name of religion. As the early church began to ally itself with state power, a countermovement simultaneously gained strength – that of hermitism, the retreat of Christian women and men to the desert in a radical rejection of money and power. Indeed, it was precisely at the time of the Crusades, in the High Middle Ages, that a man called Francis of Assisi went, as an unarmed messenger, to the camp of the Muslim sultan in an attempt to bring about peace.

It remains a huge challenge for the church to preach and practice the gospel of overcoming evil with nonviolence and reconciliation – a fact which only enhances my respect for Middle Eastern Christians who have remained true to this message in desperate circumstances. Their witness – their martyrdom – is a precious thing.

The day after Christmas, 2015, I lead the service in our local church. December 26 is traditionally a day when we remember Saint Stephen, the first Christian martyr. Stephen belonged to Jesus' group of disciples, for which he was stoned to death by Jewish fanatics around AD 36 or 40 (Acts 6–7). This year, I am uneasy about using the word "martyr," which has since acquired new connotations. Originally, it simply meant "witness" – a person who suffers a violent death for Christ's sake is a "blood witness" – and was an honorary title first bestowed on Polycarp of Smyrna in the second century. The title of martyr came with distinct conditions: firstly, the martyrdom should not be self-chosen and, secondly, Christians should *submit* to violence but never inflict it on their opponents. They pray for their persecutors – that is, they don't give up on them but hope for God's forgiveness and mercy for them too.

The ultimate example of Christian martyrdom is Jesus himself. He was willing to die for those who persecuted him, even praying for his executioners, "Father, forgive them, for they do not know what they are doing" (Luke 23:34). And Stephen emulated Jesus in death by praying similarly for his murderers, "Lord, do not hold this sin against them" (Acts 7:60). For a long time, the church adhered to the rule that only an unarmed person who suffers a violent death without inflicting violence themselves, thereby following Jesus' example, can be considered a martyr. These are the real heroes, who, instead of yielding to the blind mechanism of retaliation by hitting out at others, triumph over themselves and their vengeful instincts.

Over the course of history, the term "martyr" has become devalued by overuse. But even the Crusaders, who went to war with the pope's blessing, were denied the privilege promised to all Muslim religious fighters – they could not be revered as martyrs when they fell in battle.

In Islam, a martyr is defined very differently – he carries a weapon and dies as a holy warrior. To confer the title of martyr on fighters who have spilt the blood of others gives violence an aura of sacredness. Instead of breaking the spiral of violence, it lends it religious support. For Islamic authorities to describe suicide attacks as acts of martyrdom, in which the perpetrators go straight to paradise and their victims straight to hell, seems nothing short of perverse. This ideological reinterpretation even contradicts the Islamic legal tradition, which prohibits suicide.

A glance at our newspapers illustrates this linguistic confusion: the term "martyr" is often used for suicide bombers or terrorists who shed blood with the cry of "Allahu akbar!" The word "martyr," once the definition of a nonviolent stance, has been twisted into the exact opposite, becoming a badge of honor for misguided fanatics who seek to kill as many people as possible using weapons or explosive belts.

This is the point I attempt to make in my Saint Stephen's Day sermon: as Christians, when we speak of martyrdom, we mean exactly the opposite of what many now associate with the word. Christian martyrdom means the willingness to stand up peacefully for our beliefs, and in extreme cases to die for them – indeed, even to pray for our persecutors as we do so.

18

Easter Comes Early

Good Friday 2016. Central to the liturgy is the reading of
the Lord's Passion and the veneration of the cross. A curious
ritual, the worship of an instrument of torture! Once again,
the relationship between religion and violence is brought
home to me – the cross is a reminder that Jesus was accused
by the pious of his day; his death sentence was demanded
"for God's sake."

Many who decorate their home with a crucifix or wear
a cross around their neck perhaps do so without really
thinking about the brutality of the crucifixion, let alone
the fact that it was performed in the name of religion. But
every cross is a painful reminder of what people are capable
of inflicting on one another, and this in God's name! So, is
the charge that religion is a major cause of human violence
justified? Indeed, doesn't the image of a cross only serve to
glorify that violence? In my Good Friday sermon, I explore
some possible answers to these questions:

> The cross is a shocking reminder of what humans are
> capable of. But it is also an illustration of what Jesus was
> capable of: instead of avenging the violence inflicted on
> him, he endured it. He literally practiced what he preached:
> "Blessed are the meek"; "If anyone slaps you on the right
> cheek, turn the other cheek also." This doesn't mean that
> aggression or abuse should be passively accepted. Rather,

turning the other cheek is a nonviolent provocation that
seeks to make the aggressor aware of their own aggression.
Jesus is appealing here to the good in people, which he
believes in resolutely. As such, violence is endured in the
hope that it will run its course. In this way, old mechanisms
can be overcome. That is what redemption is: the act of
freeing the world from the constraints of the narrative of
violence.

Admittedly, it takes a lot of inner strength to choke back
our anger. It takes courage to extend the hand of reconciliation without knowing how the other person will react. But
only then can the deadly cycle of revenge be broken.

Jesus casts out the image of God the avenger. Because
Jesus' God is not a god who wished for the death of his son.
Rather, he is a friend of life – whereas we humans are often
unaccepting and incapable of that friendship.

But God bears with us: Jesus remains committed to love,
even when exposed to the full force of hatred. He rejects
the sword that one of his disciples reaches for in order to
defend his master by force. Instead of seeking to retaliate,
Jesus prays for his tormentors. He refuses to be drawn into
the spiral of hatred, but remains true to the end to God,
his fellow human beings, and himself. And so a line is
drawn under the endless catalog of revenge. Therefore the
veneration of the cross is not a glorification of violence. It is
not violence that is glorified, but Jesus himself, because he
conquers violence, overcoming it with mercy and love.

In our world, violence is glorified. And history is written
by the conquerors. Various cultures throughout the world
have erected triumphant victory monuments. The cross, on
the other hand, lays bare the conquerors' violence and lies.
The cross is the first monument in the history of humanity
to commemorate a victim. That's why Christianity has
played a part in ensuring that victims are not forgotten, and
that memorials are erected to fallen soldiers, for instance, or

to the victims of the Holocaust. The cross is the first monument to remind humanity that victims are not forgotten by God. God is not complicit in the conquerors' actions, but shows mercy to their victims. And he sees to it that they do not die in vain. After all the violence we humans inflict on each other, and even after death, God retains the last word. And that word is a word of life.

Let us therefore contemplate the crucified Christ, who overcame evil with mercy and generosity, with nonviolence and forgiveness, with friendship and love. And let us emulate and worship that figure on the cross.

Kneeling before the cross, I call to mind the many tales of endured violence I have heard over the last few months – and the many women and men who, in spite of it all, have no thought of revenge. As I kiss the cross, a shiver runs down my spine.

After the Good Friday service, I cycle over to Grünau-North. Another family from Mosul moved in there a couple of weeks ago, and I would like to discuss registering their little girl, Suhayla, for kindergarten. Besides their daughter, Shatha and her husband, Nasir, also have three sons, two of whom are already grown up, and Boulos, who is just thirteen. I was recently alerted to the family by my friend Yousif.

I ring the bell. A man of around fifty opens the door and invites me into the living room. With his shiny bald head and round figure, Nasir makes a congenial impression. The equally round Shatha hastens to serve hot tea and cookies on a low glass table. As Good Friday is a day of fasting for Catholics, I haven't eaten anything so far and gobble one cookie after another while fishing in my bag for a form and starting to enter a few details. Boulos sits next to me, acting

as interpreter. His curly black hair is cut short and he looks
at me attentively with warm, dark eyes.

Once I have gathered all the details, I sit back, and a
request springs spontaneously to my lips: "I don't know
anything about you yet. Tell me your story."

Nasir starts to talk and Boulos translates, though he
soon takes over the narrative without waiting for his father's
prompts. By now, Boulos's older brothers have joined us,
and add their own contributions to their brother's account.

The family, it seems, lived in Mosul for generations,
and belongs to the Syriac Orthodox Church. Like his
father, grandfather, and ancestors before them, Nasir is a
carpenter – an occupation as old as Christianity itself – and
ran a small, flourishing family business in Mosul. In 2003,
the Americans took the metropolis almost without a fight,
but fanatical Muslim movements were busy organizing an
underground resistance which made a point of targeting
local Christians.

One fateful morning, Nasir found a threatening letter
stuck to his front door containing a blunt demand for
money. The sum was so high that Nasir wasn't able to raise
it immediately. A few days later, his brother was stopped
in the street by jihadists and forced at gunpoint to show
his passport. Seeing the word "Christian," they opened fire
without further comment and killed him with five bullets to
the head, his six-year-old boy standing by.

Nasir knew he had to get himself and his family to
safety as quickly as possible. But he wasn't quick enough.
The very next day, masked men burst into his workshop,
firing indiscriminately. Nasir had a young son, Nimrod,
who happened to be celebrating his seventh birthday that
day and was playing in the adjacent timber yard. When the
first shot was fired, Nasir instinctively threw himself to
the ground behind the counter. The terrorists then left the

shop through the yard, from where a loud crash was heard, followed by a high-pitched scream – a death scream. Nasir rushed into the yard to find that the terrorists had knocked over a pile of heavy planks, burying the little boy beneath them.

Nasir gets out his smartphone and searches for a picture. I wince to see the little boy's face beaming back at me from the photo.

"That's Nimrod," says Boulos. And I can see the tears welling up in Nasir's eyes. I shouldn't have asked about their story, I think to myself uncomfortably. There is an oppressive silence in the room, and the family's grief is palpable. Good Friday feels very real.

We sit there in silence for a long time, and I continue gazing at the smiling child in the picture. Then I pass the phone back to Nasir and Boulos resumes his tale.

The crushed body of little Nimrod was buried the very same day at one of Mosul's Christian cemeteries. Afterward, Nasir and the heavily pregnant Shatha packed the bare essentials, loaded them into their van, and left their home city in the middle of the night with their three remaining children.

The family managed to enter Syria and settle in Qamishli, where they were relatively safe. A neighbor sent Nasir some photos of their home, which had been plundered by the jihadists. The blinds had been ripped out of their brackets and the window panes shattered. In front of the house lay a heap of wrecked furniture, torn clothing, smashed crockery, timbers, and glass fragments. One photo hit them like a punch in the stomach, showing the charred remains of oil paintings and drawings which Rami – Shatha's eldest son, and a talented artist – had had to leave behind. For Islamic fundamentalists, it is a crime to paint religious pictures or even human portraits. Another photo showed the workshop where the woodworking machinery had stood, now completely empty.

The family lived in exile in Qamishli for four years. There were five – and soon six – of them in one room, and they slept two to a bed. Nasir worked on building sites as a laborer, and the children went to a school with fifty children to a class. The two oldest boys had to work after school in a bar and restaurant to supplement their father's meager wages.

Then, five years ago, the war reached Syria. Radical Islamic fighters threatened the Christians' last remaining safe havens, such as Damascus, Aleppo, Hassake, and Homs, and fanatical religious fighters appeared in Qamishli too.

The couple knew they couldn't stay in Syria with their children any longer. Nasir made a brief last visit to Mosul. He wanted to see their house again, and Boulos went with him. In the timber yard, they found the dark, encrusted stain on the floor. Boulos can no longer remember his brother, except for this – a dried pool of blood. This was their last image of Mosul as they left the city for good.

The family managed to flee over the border into Jordan, where Nasir left his wife and children in a refugee camp before attempting to make his way to Europe with the aid of traffickers. By selling his van and all the remaining valuables, he was able to raise nine thousand dollars. He was then smuggled via Syria to Turkey in a truck, and from there across the water to Greece, hidden in the ship's engine room with six others. From Piraeus, he embarked on a long journey, often walking for days on end. Sometimes, he was able to hitch a lift for part of the way, and at the borders he was always lucky enough to find someone who could point him to suitable back roads.

Once in Germany, Nasir applied for asylum. It meant waiting for months – and in a foreign country with such a crackjaw language. Then there were all the complicated papers that had to be filled in. And the endless, helpless waiting. After six months, the news he was waiting for finally arrived: Nasir's status as an asylum seeker was recognized and he was able to bring his family over.

For a year, the six of them lived in a one-room apartment in Grünau-South. How often they thought of the big stone house they had lost, probably forever! Then recently, they finally got the chance to move into this five-room apartment. They are still getting used to living in the thin-walled prefab. The upstairs neighbor has evidently turned out to be an intimidating busybody. On one recent occasion when things got a bit noisy, he rang the bell and threatened to have the family thrown out of Germany. I attempt to allay their fears. There is one final question that interests me, and I turn to Rami, Nasir's eldest son: "What do you think of IS?"

Without hesitation, he replies, "They are blind. They think they are serving God by killing others. I love all human beings. It makes me sad."

Nasir wants to ask me a question, too: "A couple of Syriac Orthodox families have started a community in Leipzig. We're looking for a church or community center where we can meet regularly and hold services. Can you help us?"

I nod – in fact I already have an idea.

Nasir warms to his theme. "We have been driven out. But we will regroup."

This remark gets me thinking. What could be more in keeping with the spirit of Easter than to gather? After his resurrection, Jesus brought the disciples who had dispersed on Good Friday back together again in what was to be the first church – that was Easter. And these descendants of the first Christians, scattered to the four winds, are now gathering again here in Leipzig. An hour ago, I was looking at the photo of little Nimrod, the very essence of Good Friday. And now, Easter has arrived.

Shatha emerges from the kitchen and summons us to the table, where steaming, fragrant bowls announce a lavish supper. I had intended to fast today, but now we are celebrating the resurrection, and I dig in with relish. On leaving, I learn the Arabic Paschal greeting: "Al massih kam! – Christ is risen!" And the answer: "Hakan kam! – Truly, he is risen!"

A huge, cube-shaped building. Exotic music drifts out into the street, attracting the attention of passersby. An elderly couple enters the room. They are typical Leipzigers, with no religious connections. "What's going on here?" they ask. At the front, a couple of bearded men in ceremonial robes. The women's heads covered with lace scarves. And Middle Eastern song resounding from a chorus of throats.

I am standing near the entrance. "Is it a mosque?" the couple ask.

I point to the giant cross adorning the otherwise bare wall at the far end of the room. It is decorated with colorful red and yellow ornaments. "You'd be unlikely to find a cross in a mosque – this is a Christian church."

The visitors are incredulous. "And this is where Muslims hold their service?"

"No, these aren't Muslims. As you can see, men and women are singing together, in alternate choirs. These are Christians from Iraq and Syria."

"So they have converted from Islam to Christianity?"

I am struck yet again by how little we Europeans know of the history of Christians in the Middle East.

"Christianity comes from the East, and predates Islam by far. And despite a lot of problems and discrimination there are still Christian communities in Iraq and Syria today. But many of them have had to flee because they were terrorized by the Islamic State."

The two elderly visitors thank me and sit down on a pew,
visibly fascinated by the Syriac liturgy. The altar is covered
with a bright red cloth embroidered with a gold chalice
and dove motif. A silver dove is also embroidered on the
red robe of the bearded priest – a symbol of the Holy Spirit
through which Christ is made present in bread and wine
in this ritual of unity. Resting against the choir wall are
two rods with shiny silver disks on top. Two young men in
white robes pick up the rods and shake them until the tiny
bells on the disks fill the room with a high-pitched tinkling
sound. Clouds of incense rise toward the light penetrating
the church from above, and pervade the room with an
exotic, intoxicating scent. Incense from the East – a sensory
reminder of a distant homeland. I immerse myself in the
spectacle of flowing robes and echoing song, punctuated
with the Aramaic greeting of peace: "Shlomo!" I look across
at my friends from Aleppo, the families from Hassake, and
the women from Mosul, their stories of intimidation, fear,
and expulsion vividly before my eyes. And I think of the
churches of the East and how much suffering and persecution they have had to endure. The fervent prayer for peace
does indeed have a special place and resonance in their
liturgy.

Among those attending this Syriac Orthodox service are
also members of the (Egyptian) Coptic Church, Greek
Orthodox and Armenian Christians, Protestant nuns, and
Catholics who have made their way to this newly built
Catholic church. This really is ecumenism in action: Christians from north and south, east and west coming together
around the same altar to pray for the peace of Christ.

When Yousif had to state Amanuel's religion on his
school registration form a couple of months ago, he

unhesitatingly wrote "Christian." In the secretary's office, they wanted to know whether the boy was Protestant or Catholic. Yousif was quick with his answer: "Was Jesus Catholic or Protestant?" I followed this up by explaining that Amanuel was a Christian from Iraq and simply wanted to participate in religious education lessons, irrespective of denomination.

I think back to the fourteen-year-old Ayad, and to Nasir's brother, both of whom were made to present their passports to the jihadists in Iraq. The word printed there was "Christian," and it was for that that they were both killed on the spot. They and many others like them have borne witness to the faith with their blood, and their fate demonstrates only too well that what matters is the fact of being a *Christian*. All denominational, linguistic, or cultural distinctions fade into insignificance before the deaths suffered for the sake of Jesus Christ. It is of no interest to the terrorists whether their victims belong to an Orthodox or Western church.

A person becomes Christian through baptism, connecting them to Jesus Christ through immersion in his life, death, and resurrection. And regardless of the different denominations, whether Catholic, Protestant, or Syriac Orthodox, baptism is recognized by all as the crucial sign of belonging to the *one church of Jesus Christ*.

There is a sad chapter of church history that fills me with grief and shame, namely the attempts by the Roman Catholic Church to "evangelize" the Syriac churches, or in other words to subjugate them to a Western theology and church structure. In the nineteenth century, the patriarch of the mountain Assyrians lamented that his church was suffering under two Muhammads, the "Muhammad of the East" (the prophet of Islam) and the "Muhammad of the West," meaning the pope in Rome, whose missionaries

had weakened his small church and accelerated its
decline by causing it to splinter. Indeed, libraries that had
survived all the looting by Arabs, Turks, and Kurds were
ultimately destroyed by Catholic missionaries from the
West – theological know-it-alls who looked down on the
riches of Eastern theology with contempt. Sadly, the Protestant churches took a similar line, and it is Protestant groups
which are most keen to "convert" Eastern Christians today,
thus contributing to further splits.

This fragmentation has had a damaging effect on the
churches of the Middle East, causing their message to
become obscured. If a Muslim wants to become a Christian
today, for example, they first have to have the complicated
denominational differences explained to them.

In light of the martyrdom of many Eastern Christians
and the annihilation of whole churches, the time is surely
ripe to push ahead boldly with the project of ecumenism.
The differences between the churches are something to be
treasured and preserved. And when believers of diverse
denominations seal their Christian testimony with their own
blood, shouldn't we then celebrate the unity Christ gives
us through his body – that is, the church – in communion,
where we all share in the body and blood of Christ?

In his high-profile speech upon receiving the 2015 Peace
Prize of the German Book Trade, Navid Kermani drew
attention to the neglect of Eastern Christians by their
Western counterparts, citing the priest Jacques Mourad's
words, "We mean nothing to them." This warning from a
Muslim to us Christians to wake up at last to the plight
of our threatened and oppressed brethren must surely
shake us out of our complacency. Perhaps the West's long
indifference to the fate of Eastern Christians has made the
Islamic forces even more ruthless. Given the West's failure

to stand up for either the Armenians or the Arameans,
why shouldn't they go ahead and slaughter or expel the last
Christians from the Middle East as well?

It is high time for us to respond to Kermani's wake-up
call. Eastern Christians deserve our full solidarity. Since
they have now been dispersed worldwide, we could make it
our mission to seek them out, make contact with them, and
invite them into our communities.

- We can approach reception camps, advice centers, and aid
  agencies in order to locate Middle Eastern Christians and
  offer them practical assistance with finding accommodation
  and work.

- In the case of individuals or families, inviting them to
  join our local churches would be an important gesture
  of fellowship. Eastern Christians come with the precious
  heritage of their faith, their church, and their history.
  Another possibility is to invite them to participate in our
  church services, for instance, by leading the Lord's Prayer
  in Aramaic, particularly during the main festivals of the
  church calendar.

- If a sizeable group of Eastern Christians can be assem-
  bled in a town, we can help them set up a community by
  offering them our church facilities. That way we can support
  their efforts to practice the faith that caused them to be
  expelled in the first place, and to keep their traditions alive.
  A concerted attempt by church schools to take Christian
  children from the Middle East can also help further this
  initiative.

The Eastern churches, descended in a direct line from the
original church, are being scattered around the globe. Some
of them are perhaps doomed to die out, and if so, Jesus'
words may prove true: "Unless a kernel of wheat falls to the

ground and dies, it remains only a single seed. But if it dies, it produces many seeds" (John 12:24).

Out of the painful fragmentation of the Eastern churches a new fruitfulness can come, for they bring with them a precious heritage, and if that heritage is valued and accepted by the Western churches, the traditions of the East will live on. The Roman Catholic Church in particular, which draws so heavily on traditions, could become the mother of all traditional churches if it were to adopt and integrate the legacy of the East. To cite a few examples:

- The Eastern churches were both *missionary and dialogical.* They valued the cultures of Asia and engaged in a dynamic intellectual exchange with Buddhism and Hinduism. They also helped to shape Islam by imparting important philosophical and scientific knowledge to the Muslim cultural sphere. Fortunately, inculturation and dialogue with other religions and belief systems have played a central role in Roman Catholicism since the establishment of the Second Vatican Council. But there are also traditionalist schools of thought that seek to turn the clock back. We only need to look at the churches of the Middle East to see the value of interaction with other religions.

- Since ancient times, the Eastern churches have – in the midst of a patriarchal society – accorded *women* a place both in the liturgy and church administration. The office of deaconess, whose duties revolved around adult baptism and teaching, was open to women, for example, while abbesses deputized for the bishop in distributing communion. This age-old tradition still persists in the Eastern church, and provides a solid foundation on which to progress toward equality for women in the church.

- The Syriac churches have also, from their earliest days, accorded *equal respect to monastic celibacy and marriage* – including in the case of married priests. Similarly, their reasonable and sensitive approach to various problematic pastoral issues could be adopted and continued within the Roman Catholic Church.

• Eastern Christians have, within a predominantly Muslim environment, remained true to their faith and kept it alive over many centuries. Today, Christianity is likewise moving toward a *minority status* in Western countries. Therefore we can learn from our Eastern counterparts how to practice our faith with dedication and fortitude as a minority.

• Amid the decline and perhaps even disappearance of the Syriac churches, we mustn't forget their witness to the early Christian stance of *nonviolence.* Over many centuries, Christians in the East have remained true to Jesus and the gospel in this respect and borne witness with their blood, while those in Byzantium and Rome have yielded to the temptations of state power. The legacy of nonviolence is Jesus' central bequest to his church. The churches of the Middle East continue to remind us of this legacy, which can be asserted and built on in the churches of the West. The church owes this much to its founder and to the world of today. In light of the violence allegedly committed in God's name, it is vitally important to proclaim the gospel and its conciliatory power with *one* voice. And when the spirit of nonviolence comes to illuminate the doctrine and practice of the Western churches, then the churches of the East can truly be said to have risen again in them.

19

Giving of Our Best

Many people from Syria and Iraq have had to give up everything and flee to the West in peril of their lives. Erecting walls against refugees is an act of cynicism. To let people starve or freeze to death outside our borders would be to destroy the fundamental values on which our society is founded.

At the same time, it is clear that the influx of refugees is set to bring about a radical change in our society. We are at a crossroads: either we succeed in integrating those refugees into our society and value system – in which case everyone wins. Or we duck the challenges and retreat into nationalist ideologies – in which case everyone loses.

Countless people – Christians and Muslims alike – are fleeing to Europe to escape the terror of Islamism. The chaotic conditions in their native countries have plunged people of various religions into terrible misery. Now they are in search of a new home, but also different political systems and social values: human rights and democracy, women's rights and gender equality, religious freedom and tolerance. The great challenge facing our Western society is to win them over to these values. If we welcome the displaced in a spirit of openness, they will come to know and appreciate our values.

1. Separation of State and Religion

From its beginnings, Christianity has challenged the use of violence in the name of God: belief in God is a matter of individual conscience and conditional upon freedom. As the North African theologian Tertullian (ca. 160–220) wrote, "It is no part of religion to compel religion – to which free will and not force should lead us."

After Emperor Constantine recognized Christianity as the state religion, its original distance from state power was lost. As a result, the use of armed force and the persecution of people of other faiths began to be justified on religious grounds. One of the achievements of the Enlightenment was to push for the separation of state and religion, partly in response to the terrible acts of violence that had been committed "in the name of God." This paved the way for the development of a secular state which was no longer tied to a particular denomination or religion, and thus able to guarantee equal rights and religious freedom for all citizens.

Though already enshrined in the gospel and the practice of the early church, it was only after a long process of self-purification that this separation was recognized again by the Roman Catholic Church, for example. This sometimes bitter learning experience is something which the churches could bring to bear in modern-day interfaith dialogues with Islam.

After all, many Muslims are well aware that, in its current state, Islam suffers from too close a connection between religion and state. This unhappy entanglement is one of the causes of a long history of excessive violence stretching into the present. The Islamic State is just one of many examples of the wicked barbarity into which human beings can stray if they elevate one particular religion to a position of absolute authority over all political and social questions.

Sadly, Western states have lost their credibility in the Arab world far too often. It was all too obvious, for instance, that America's "liberation" of Iraq wasn't just about the introduction of democratic values and human rights, but first and foremost about economic interests. On my visit to Ankawa, one question came up time after time: With so many dictatorships in the world, why did the United States choose to remove Saddam Hussein? The answer, clearly, was that he ruled over a country with huge oil resources. The hypocrisy of Western politics is exemplified by its readiness to make alliances with regressive Islamic regimes. States such as Saudi Arabia or Qatar, which cling to an ossified form of Islam, are supplied with arms which they use to strengthen and expand their regime. The ideologies of Al-Qaeda, IS, and Boko Haram have been well greased with huge sums of money from the oil wells of the Gulf States. Saudi Arabia in particular has been pouring oil onto the fire of Islamic fundamentalism for decades. Thousands of mosques and tens of thousands of preachers have been exported throughout the world to promote the state-endorsed Islamic sect of Wahhabism and suppress Muslim reform movements. When it comes to taking in refugees from Syria or even giving financial support to refugee relief schemes, the Saudis are remarkably reticent, yet they are only too keen to invest money in the construction of mosques in Germany in order to promote the further spread of their intolerant version of Islam. In spite of all this, Saudi Arabia continues to be treated as a great ally by the United States, and the same is true of Germany. Once again, it seems, Western values and democratic principles are being swept under the carpet to safeguard economic interests. Such ambivalence makes a mockery of Western politicians' claims to champion democracy and human rights.

Large numbers of victims of the wars stirred up by Islamic fundamentalism are now coming to our countries. The majority of the refugees are Muslims. Many of them have also been ideologically poisoned by decades of propaganda claiming that Christians are "impure," that the West is morally corrupt, and that only Muslims can be citizens in the full sense of the word.

Now there is a chance for Muslim refugees to encounter the positive achievements of Western states for themselves. As Muslims, they are recognized as equal before the state law; this experience may change the way they think and win them over to an alternative model of state and religion in which the two are strictly segregated. Such a learning process cannot happen overnight. Moreover, the unity of religion and state is deeply rooted in Islam's DNA – in the Koran and the example of the Prophet Muhammad. But there are also Muslim thinkers who seek to reconcile the separation of state and religion with the religious tradition of Islam. Such interpretations deserve our full sympathy and support. Indeed, the fact that many Muslims are now suffering as a result of the explosive mix of religion and politics and fleeing the terror of the fundamentalists may present a window of opportunity, encouraging greater openness to the possibility of a differently founded society, and an appreciation of the theory and practice of a secular state model.

2. In Praise of Pluralism

All social, religious, or political movements stem from a strong need for community and unity. Jesus chose a group of twelve apostles from among his disciples who – reflecting the twelve tribes of Israel – symbolized the unity of the new community.

But whenever people come together in groups – religious or secular – the question of the relationship between unity and diversity always arises. Early Christianity faced its first acid test when tensions arose between Christians with Jewish roots and those who had previously belonged to a "heathen" religion. Following major conflicts, the so-called Apostolic Council agreed on a policy of unity in diversity: the Jewish Christians recognized Jesus as the Messiah while remaining true to Jewish dietary rules and the tradition of circumcision; the "heathen Christians" also believed in Jesus Christ, but they were not obliged to observe the Jewish law. In later centuries, peaceable agreement on church issues was often no longer possible, as the profession of Christianity had become politicized under the Roman-Byzantine Empire. Debates between theologians could escalate into civil wars. As a result, the Roman emperors sought to impose one particular interpretation of the Christian faith, if necessary by force. The fragmentation of Christianity into different denominations was therefore not only a matter of theology, but also politics.

The ecumenical movement of recent decades has led to a rediscovery of the rich diversity maintained through the different denominations. The desire to return to the original church has also proved conducive to the recognition of legitimate diversity. Indeed, Christianity's founding document is itself pluralist: there are four Gospels which already reflect four different traditions and interpretations based on the writers' experiences of Jesus Christ and his impact on their lives. The result is a justifiable plurality of denominations which have grown with our culture and history and can have a mutually enriching effect.

The strength of original Islam lay in the great unity which the new faith was able to bring about between the estranged

Bedouin tribes of Arabia. The dispute over Muhammad's legitimate successor already began at his deathbed, however, and this issue has divided Islam ever since. The conflict between Sunnis and Shiites is still being played out to this day with often brutal violence.

The Islamic State's aim is to restore the original unity that the Prophet Muhammad succeeded in establishing between the Arabian tribes. Part of the appeal of IS lies in this vision, which projects the ideal Islamic state of the early days of Muhammad into the present, seeking to unite Muslims once again in a single faith under the leadership of a spiritual and political ruler (caliph).

The vision of a strictly unified Islamic state is, however, an illusion. Islam has never been a homogenous structure since its foundation. The more this Arabian tribal religion spread to new cultural circles, the more it diversified. Contact with Syriac Christianity – and through it, ancient Greek philosophy – and intermingling with Persian and Indian religions led to the emergence of many varieties of Islam. Many traditions fed into Islam, creating a broad spectrum of denominations, from the Alawites to Sufi-influenced folk religion. The different denominations were often locked in bitter conflict, however, and these intra-Islamic differences are one reason for the rampant violence currently afflicting Syria.

If Muslim refugees are taken in by our Western society in large numbers, there is a chance that they will learn to appreciate pluralism and the notion that different Muslim denominations and traditions can coexist harmoniously. As in Christian ecumenism, intra-Muslim diversity could come to be valued as an asset – and as a stage along the path to recognition of the pluralism of religions (including atheism) in general. Such an approach can be practically applied through *interfaith dialogue*, where the parties are

able to engage on a level playing field. In this way, age-old
behavioral patterns that label people of other faiths as
unbelievers or as inferior can be erased. Interfaith dialogue
that helps overcome false claims to exclusivity is a thorn
in the fundamentalists' side; it is no coincidence that IS
destroyed the seventeen-hundred-year-old Mar Elian
monastery in Syria, which made a point of cultivating
such exchanges. That crime should spur us on to even
greater efforts to promote the interaction of Christians and
Muslims.

3. Religious Freedom and Tolerance

Having suffered persecution from the outset, the Christian
church fought to achieve religious freedom. As soon as
it came to power, however, the tables were turned. In the
West, the main victims were the Jews, suffering centuries
of discrimination. A religiously motivated anti-Semitism
found a foothold in some scriptures of the New Testament,
reflecting as they did the oppression of the first Christians by Jewish authorities. After much prevarication, the
churches of the West have finally begun to address the
anti-Semitic elements in their history, and theology and
church practice have since succeeded in developing a new
relationship with Judaism as the "older sibling." At the
same time, a new recognition of religious freedom has been
achieved.

At the beginning of his mission, Muhammad was well
disposed toward Jews and Christians. For one thing, the
prophet – whether consciously or unconsciously – borrowed
much of the content of the Koran from the two older faiths.
Secondly, he was keen to win Jews and Christians over to
his new religion. It is to this early period of Islam, when

Muhammad was active in Mecca, that the Koran's positive statements about both faiths can be attributed.

When many Jews and Christians refused to recognize Muhammad as the definitive prophet of God, however, he began to adopt a more aggressive tone. And since, according to current interpretations, the later revelations (of Medina) cancel out the earlier ones, the suras that laid the foundations of today's anti-Christian ideology tend to prevail.

As we can see, the Koranic scriptures contain an element of ambivalence. Although there is a certain respect toward Jews and Christians as "possessors of a holy book," they are also accused of falsehood. In practice, this has led followers of both religions to be regarded as fundamentally inferior members of society in all Islamic-led political systems to date. Ingrained over centuries, these discriminatory practices run deep and are constantly being fueled in Islamic countries through preaching and social practice. From an early age, children are indoctrinated with contempt for "impure Christians" through schoolbooks and songs. To give another example, in December 2015, imams in Baghdad banned their followers from wishing their (last remaining) Christian neighbors a Merry Christmas.

For the Christian church, the genocide of the Jews in the Third Reich was among a number of factors prompting it to take a long, hard look at the anti-Semitic elements in its own tradition. Sadly, the Muslim genocide of Christian peoples which preceded it, and indeed provided a model for it, has produced no such effect. To this day, Turkey continues to deny the genocide of the Armenians, Greeks, and Arameans. But failing to face up to its complicity only encourages further religiously motivated violence. In this way, Turkey, among others, has paved the way for similar crimes in the name of Islam to be repeated – with similar savagery – in the twenty-first century.

The pattern has remained the same for centuries: a holy war is declared on "unbelievers," and those branded as such are expelled or deemed eligible for execution. Violent attacks against Christians with the aim of "converting" them to Islam or driving them out are now once again the norm in all Islamic countries. A striking feature is the extent to which religious leaders incite their followers to looting and violence through a constant barrage of hate preaching. To cite another recent, crass example, the Salafist sheik Yasir al-Ajlawni of Damascus issued a fatwa on April 5, 2013, stating that it was not against the laws of Islam to rape Christian women.

In some countries, the looting and burning of Christian houses by Muslim mobs after Friday prayer is almost commonplace. The fact that hate preachers are trained and funded by states that are on the best economic terms with the West is one of the grossest political perversions of the last few decades.

Even here, however, there is a glimmer of hope on the horizon. Many Muslim states have made commitments – on paper – to human rights and religious freedom. In those countries, Christian victims of discrimination can therefore, at least in theory, assert their rights in court. While this will not always succeed in practice, a steady insistence on chartered rights may help bring about a change in the Muslim population's sense of justice. This will take time and patience, and above all support from Western media and social networks engaged in human rights campaigns.

Another encouraging sign was the Marrakesh Declaration of January 2016, in which 250 imams and legal

scholars from Shiite and Sunni states condemned all forms
of discrimination against non-Muslims in Islamic countries. They called for a concept of citizenship that gives
equal space to other religions and cultures. And finally,
they demanded that all discriminatory statements against
non-Muslims be removed from school curriculums.

Even if these Islamic scholars only constitute a small
minority within the Muslim world, we must take them
at their word and offer them our support. Muslims who
are longstanding European residents have a key role to
play as well: they can share their positive experiences of
a democratic and tolerant society with Muslim refugees
and so help to overcome the deep-seated attitude of "anti-
Christianism." European Islamic associations can lend their
support to democratic movements in Islamic countries,
while Muslims in Europe can call for the same freedoms
they enjoy here, such as the freedom to build mosques, to
be granted to Christians in Turkey. It was in this spirit that
the German Green party chairman Cem Özdemir spoke
out in the spring of 2016 against Turkey's nationalization of
Christian churches.

Europe has a duty to give the best of what its history has to
offer: human rights, democracy, gender equality, the rule
of law, and religious freedom. Only if Muslims feel that
they are treated fairly and equitably can minds begin to
be changed. Attacks on Muslims, even if "only" verbal, are
disastrous, serving to deepen the old prejudices and divi-
sions. Conversely, a welcoming culture should not lead us to
sweep our own culture under the prayer mat. Why should
school meals be made halal across the board, for example?
To suddenly impose Muslim dietary rules on non-Muslims
sends out the wrong signal, by endorsing Muslims' claims to

religious superiority and cementing the devaluation of other faiths. Even if it adds to the financial and organizational burden, offering a choice makes pluralism and equality a practical reality. Pork or pork-free: that is the question – and so it should remain!

It will take time for some Christians from Iraq and Syria to be reconciled with Muslims after having been shamefully betrayed by their Muslim neighbors. The injuries they and their ancestors have suffered over centuries run deep. Yet instead of preaching hatred, they pray for peace and reconciliation. And if the Marrakesh Declaration proves to be more than mere lip service, respectful and friendly relations between Eastern Christians and Muslims will be able to grow again on a new and sustainable basis. I think with admiration of Rami from Mosul, whose younger brother was murdered by the jihadists and whose Christian family was driven from their home: now he is giving up his time to accompany a Muslim family on visits to the authorities as a volunteer interpreter.

The abandonment of the term "unbeliever" and the mentality associated with it poses major theological challenges for Islam. It means interpreting the Koran in such a way that followers are guided not by the later suras, but the revelations from the early period. While such a reading contradicts many classical currents within Islam, it has been well argued by many Muslim theologians. The courageous book by Mouhanad Khorchide, *Gott glaubt an den Menschen* ("God Believes in Human Beings"), highlights the fact that Islamic theology since Muhammad's Medina period has, on many occasions, served to justify violent opposition to people of different beliefs. Such self-critical analysis can help Islam to free itself from the patterns of violence which grew out of a specific political situation, the military conflicts in Medina.

Other contemporary Muslim thinkers are similarly engaged in seeking arguments for a pluralist constitutional state in the Koran. They point, for instance, to the fact that the call to belief is an appeal to individual conscience and is therefore conditional on freedom of choice – a basis from which the notion of religious freedom might perhaps be argued. Whether such readings of the Koran, which are possible at Western universities, will be accepted in Islamic countries or among the wider Muslim population is another matter.

4. Called to Common Witness
Central to interfaith dialogue is a discussion of the spiritual dimensions of the religion in question. The starting point and core of any religion is the human sense of wonder at the mystery of God – by whatever name – who will always be greater than any human concept or image. This experience can foster a profound appreciation of pluralism, illustrating that there is more than one way to God. Indeed, in the words of Pope Benedict XVI, "there are as many paths to God as there are people in the world." Such an appreciation must lead to the practice of nonviolence, as only then can the individual decide freely on their path to God.

This is probably the greatest challenge facing Islamic theology and practice, which has never at any point in its history allowed Muslims to quit their religion. Apostasy from Islam has been, and continues to be, punishable by death, and this pattern of violence has become so deeply ingrained in Islamic societies that it is often family members who are responsible for the murder of apostates.

Religiosity that is imposed by force can only command external allegiance; a religion that focuses on God must grant freedom. What matters to God is the free consent of the heart. The actions of Jesus and the heritage of the Eastern churches in particular set an example of nonviolence. Even if the fundamental sources of Islam fail to offer much criticism of violence, a few Muslim thinkers have argued for such a stance. It is high time for an alliance between such schools of thought, as only they can proclaim God's covenant with the people in a way that carries conviction.

Testifying to God is the great challenge facing modern-day Islam and Christianity alike. Because humans are made for freedom, the credibility of a religion is measured by whether it promotes and encourages human freedom. Any act of violence that is committed in the name of a religion fundamentally destroys that credibility.

Christianity and Islam must cultivate a dialogue and work hand in hand for the free exercise of religion if they are to avoid obscuring the testimony to God that is their common calling. The justification of violence by religious people has instilled in many people a suspicion of religion in general, leading them to regard it as the cause of violence and war. For many, this suspicion makes belief in God fundamentally problematic. Only when Christianity and Islam are able to come together in a practical demonstration of the peacemaking power of religion will they be able to fulfill their original mission of bearing credible witness to the God who is, in their respective faiths, synonymous with love and mercy.

Epilogue

....

The Gift of Home

For nearly a year now, Peter has been coming to Amanuel and Shaba to help them with their homework. The sixteen-year-old high school student was placed with them via the Leipzig Refugee Council. Yousif tells me that Peter comes much more often than originally arranged. He evidently feels quite at ease with the family, sometimes popping over for supper and staying late. These visits are a completely new experience for Peter. His parents separated when he was young and he often felt pushed from pillar to post and not really at home anywhere. At Yousif and Tara's, he encounters the warm hospitality of an Eastern family whose door is always open and for whom it's never any trouble to set an extra place at the table. Here, Peter feels a sense of belonging, knowing that he is always welcome.

Peter has also made another discovery: like most Leipzigers, he received no religious education at school. Having grown up in an atheist environment, he doesn't believe in God. Through Tara and Yousif, he has come to know a deeply religious family: the walls are decorated with Christian symbols and grace is said before meals. Above all, however, he has discovered that belief in God is not just an intellectual exercise for Yousif and his family, but defines their whole life. They have paid a high price for their Christian faith, losing their home and all their possessions for the sake of Jesus Christ. Their faith is so infinitely important to them that they have refused to give it up at any cost. This all-engulfing devotion is not something the young Leipziger can relate to. But he understands something of its psychological importance. For these refugees, their faith is a support, buoying them up and comforting them after all the losses they have suffered. The Christian faith gives meaning to their lives. They have not become embittered by the hardships they have endured. They believe in the future, trusting that their lives are safe in the hands of a greater power.

Peter has regular discussions with Yousif or Amanuel about the existence of God. For Yousif too, this is a new experience, never having met anyone before who doesn't believe in God. Their conversations are a highly respectful – and mutually enriching – exchange between believer and nonbeliever.

My contacts with Christian refugees from the East have led me, too, to reflect about what my faith means to me. Is it just a cultural tradition, designed to dress up everyday life with a few rituals? If I take my Christianity seriously, then it has to be all or nothing. Because if this world owes its existence to God, our faith must be one that cares for the planet. If all human beings are God's children, then that faith is expressed in the quest for equality and brotherhood. At the heart of the Christian faith is the figure of Jesus Christ, in whom God's love toward humanity was revealed. And we can encounter this close and loving God by standing up for the rejected and the oppressed, the needy and the displaced, with whom God identifies through Jesus Christ: "I was a stranger and you took me in" (Matt. 25:43).

From Eastern Christians I have learned that my faith is worth denying myself for. I don't have to give up everything, thank goodness. But at the same time, I can ask myself: Can I do without luxury and excess to make room for refugees? And what priorities do I set in my free time, given that so many people have come to our country needing urgent practical help?

The same question applies to what we believe as a society. If we are really serious about peace, justice, and preserving creation, we mustn't forget that these values also have their price. Freedom and human dignity don't come free. Humanity has to be wrung out of complacency, nationalistic egoism, and consumerism. Justice cannot thrive until we abandon the fallacy of unlimited growth. Peace will not be possible until we are willing to dismantle the arms industry and stop supporting totalitarian regimes. Would I support a policy that may also impose some level of sacrifice, in the interests of a fairer economic world order? Do I support non-governmental organizations that campaign for the victims of political and economic systems?

Christians from the Middle East have given up everything in order to remain true to their belief in the gospel. They come from the homeland of Christianity and remind us of our own origins and values. By opening our doors to them, we have it in our power to preserve this precious legacy and ensure a more humane future for humanity.

Blessed are you who have left your homes and work behind to stay true to your faith. Be patient, do not lose hope amid all the trials and fears you must endure today, for I will never leave you.

Blessed are you who do not fear the loss of your homeland and possessions. You have chosen the path of refugeehood. You have chosen poverty and humiliation and have become one with me in suffering. Remain in me and you will share in the honor that comes from God.

Blessed are you who have preserved your hearts from hatred and rage. You have not fought evil with evil, that you may be children of your Father in heaven.

Blessed are you who suffer in your ravaged souls. You have been uprooted; your memories have been plundered and shattered. Know that every day of your life and every tear that you shed are preserved in God's heart.

Blessed are you who are willing to live as guests, strangers, and nomads. For you are witnesses to God's kingdom through your humility and your faith, your forgiveness and your joy.

(This text was formulated by young Christians in 2015 for a service at a refugee camp in Ankawa.)

The Author

 A poet, priest, and prolific author in Germany, Andreas Knapp left a secure position as head of Freiburg Seminary to live and work among the poor as a member of the Little Brothers of the Gospel, a religious order inspired by Charles de Foucauld. Today he shares an apartment with three brothers in Leipzig's largest housing project, and ministers to prisoners, college students, and refugees.

Other Titles from Plough

Bearing Witness: *Stories of Martyrdom
and Costly Discipleship*
Edited by Charles E. Moore and Timothy Keiderling
Stories of Christian martyrs from around the world and
through the ages to inspire and challenge the next generation
of believers.

The Early Christians: *In Their Own Words*
Eberhard Arnold
What did Christianity look like before it became an institu-
tion? Find out for yourself with this collection of firsthand
accounts of the early church. Includes excerpts from Origen,
Tertullian, Polycarp, Clement of Alexandria, Justin, Irenaeus,
and others – and equally revealing material from their critics,
detractors, and persecutors.

Jesus and the Nonviolent Revolution
André Trocmé
In this book, you'll encounter a Jesus you may have never met
before – a Jesus who not only calls for spiritual transformation,
but for practical changes that answer the most perplexing
political, economic, and social problems of our time.

Seeking Peace: *Notes and Conversations along the Way*
Johann Christoph Arnold
Where can we find peace of heart and mind – with ourselves,
with others, and with God? This book offers some surprising
answers.

The Plough Publishing House
www.plough.com, info@plough.com
151 Bowne Drive, PO BOX 398, Walden, NY 12586, USA
Brightling Road, Robertsbridge, East Sussex, TN32 5DR, UK
4188 Gwydir Highway, Elsmore NSW 2360, AU